The Book of Uncommon Prayer

Contemplative and Celebratory Prayers and Worship Services for Youth Ministry

Steven L. Case

Youth Specialties

ZONDERVAN

The Book of Uncommon Prayer: Contemplative and Celebratory Prayers and Worship Services for Youth Ministry

Copyright © 2002 by Youth Specialties

Youth Specialties Books, 300 S. Pierce St., El Cajon, CA 92020, are published by Zondervan, 5300 Patterson Ave. S.E., Grand Rapids, MI 49530.

Library of Congress Cataloging-in-Publication Data

Case, Steve, 1964—

The Book of Uncommon Prayers : contemplative and celebratory prayers and worship services for youth ministry / Steve Case.

p. cm.

Includes index.

ISBN 0-310-24142-1

1. Youth—Prayer-books and devotions—English. I. Title.

BV283.Y6 C27 2002

264'.00835—dc21

2002005434

Unless otherwise indicated, all Scripture quotations are taken from the Holy Bible: New International Version (North American Edition). Copyright © 1973, 1978, 1984 by International Bible Society. Used by permission of Zondervan Publishing House.

Web site addresses listed in this book were current at the time of publication. Please contact Youth Specialties via e-mail (YS@YouthSpecialties.com) to report URLs that are no longer operational and replacement URLs if available.

Edited by Dave Urbanski

Cover and Interior design by Proxy

Printed in the United States of America

05 06 07 / ML / 10 9 8 7 6 5

Uncommon, Indeed {5}

Daily Prayers {11}

A prayer for each day of the week...{12-15}

Services {17}

Prayers {67}

Responsive Readings {89}

Private Devotions for Youth Workers {107}

Communion/Worship Service for *Eucharist* CD {121}

Lyrics and Notes for *Eucharist* CD {125}

113404

Dedication and Acknowledgments

Dedication

This book is the fulfillment of a dream. Please do not take those words lightly. I have dreamed of being a writer. But if someone told me that the cost of publishing a book is that I spend one less moment with my wife, I would burn these files, flip burgers for a living, and never write another word for the rest of my life. As it happens, every word I write is for her, every moment I breathe is for her, and so is this book.

Acknowledgments

I would like to acknowledge the Episcopal Church and the writers of the original *Book of Common Prayer* who inspired this work.

I would like to thank the good people at Youth Specialties who saw the idea and thought it had a shot.

I would like to acknowledge all of the students at Windermere Union Church and all those others I have had over the years who put up with the insanity and allowed me to try out the ideas contained in this book.

I would like to acknowledge *The Message* author, Eugene Peterson, and the American Bible Society (CEV) who put the Scriptures in a language that even a guy like me can understand.

I would like to acknowledge Perry Ferrell, Bobby McFerrin, and Lost & Found whose music was constantly playing while this book was being created.

Uncommon, Indeed

In 1993—although I had never been a part of an Episcopal worship service—I took a youth director position for an Episcopal church.

Life (and youth ministry) can be funny that way.

While treading these new waters, this dyed-in-the-wool Methodist/Presbyterian discovered for the very first time *The Book of Common Prayer*.

In fact, I came to love it.

Pieces and variations of *The Book of Common Prayer* can be found in the hymnals and worship books of many other denominations. And it has become one of the most important tools in my ministry, next to the Bible (and caffeine, of course). I took a copy of *The Book of Common Prayer* with me when I left the Episcopal church for my next youth ministry position, and I have used it in every church I've worked in since then.

In *The Book of Common Prayer* I found morning services, evening services, communion services, and even a service for the ordination of a bishop (in case the youth group was ever confronted with a non-ordained bishop who needed our help). I also found hundreds of prayers for every occasion, responsive readings, and well-known Scriptures.

The Book of Common Prayer accompanied me on every retreat, lock-in, and mission trip. I tossed it into my Land's End bag with my Bible and folder of permission slips. It provided me with worship experiences and liturgies that helped me create wonderful "God moments" that we all want our youth to experience.

Flash forward almost a decade later.

What you are reading is the end of several years of work—*The Book of Uncommon Prayer*. Uncommon because these prayers and worship services are written for youth ministry—for teens and for youth workers! Uncommon because the words inside speak the truth…and speak it straight from the gut. No punches pulled. Uncommon because it's a prayer book and worship manual for all denominations. It doesn't matter if you're Protestant or Catholic, mainline or evangelical: in these pages you'll find worship services, prayers, readings, Scriptures, and devotions that all teenagers and youth workers in Jesus' church can enjoy and benefit from. The services are written for retreats, lock-ins— even sunrises and sunsets. There are also youth services for Christmas, Good Friday, All

Hallows Eve, and other special occasions. The prayers are written for teenagers and the obstacles and challenges they face every day.

Why Use a Book Like This?

You can put together amazing youth talks. You can lead eye-opening mission trips. But if you sat your teenagers down and asked them to remember the moments when they felt really connected to God, you'd probably get answers like—

"That night we sat in front of the fireplace..."

"When we sat on the dock and watched the sun come up and read from Genesis..."

"When we all held candles and stood on the roof and listened to that one song by..."

This book will provide the tools you need to create those wonderful God moments when teenagers suddenly become aware of the presence of the Holy Spirit.

This Book Is a Tool

Okay, it's the first day of your winter retreat. The topic for the weekend is "peer pressure."

You've got the games lined up. You have a nice couple that has volunteered to work in the kitchen. No one got lost on the way to the retreat center. The morning lesson went very well. The students are all outside sledding, and you can smell the hot cocoa beginning to warm in the kitchen. Are you the greatest youth worker in the world or what? Then you remember that you're in charge of this evening's worship service!

That's why you bought this book. (Unless you're just browsing in the bookstore racks or at a convention table, in which case you should immediately *buy* this book!)

You can turn in these pages to find a service for the close of the day—and the order of worship is right there for you. Turn to the Prayers section and choose a prayer for unity, a prayer for courage, or any other prayer that fits what you have planned for your group. Are you worshipping outside or inside? There are prayers listed for both situations.

Many of the readings are written specifically for the students to read aloud. You can pass this book around a circle or copy the prayers so everyone can participate. So...just pick some music from the CD the youth left sitting out, jot down a few ideas to use for a talk, and you're good to go!

That's why you bought this book.

There's Something for You, Too

This book also contains affirmations and prayers for your own spiritual journey. In the back, you'll find devotions and prayers written specifically for you, the youth worker. Youth ministry is a *calling*. (You probably already knew that.) No sane person would *choose* this vocation. The section titled Private Devotions for Youth Workers is for just you. It contains daily prayer guides as well as devotions, all written to renew and strengthen you for just *one more* parent meeting, *one more* performance review, *one more* day.

The *Eucharist* CD

In the back of the book is a CD called *Eucharist*. It's an ancient-postmodern collection of songs from the United Kingdom that sets the mood for communion like nothing else you've ever heard. *Eucharist* was created several years ago, specifically to guide and color the communion service at the Greenbelt Festival—the annual Christian music and arts gathering in England—and the crowd response was good enough to warrant a full-scale recording.

The CD's creators—Jonny Baker and his friends from Grace Church and other U.K. congregations—are part of a movement called "alternate worship," which is in part influenced by club (dance) culture across the pond. The sounds and artistic approaches on *Eucharist* are directly linked to this growing worship movement. (If you want to find out more about what these folks are doing, check out jonnybaker.blogspot.com)

Many of the services in this book use the songs from the *Eucharist* CD, and there's even an entire service that uses the CD from start to finish.

The Book of Uncommon Prayer is a practical tool, a source of God-revealing worship, and a guide for personal renewal.

That's why you bought this book.

Why Liturgy?

Liturgy isn't a dirty word!

For many Christians, *liturgy* is a dirty word. (Actually all it means is the rituals or "rites" of public worship—that's pretty tame!) But there are those in the church who maintain that participation in things like responsive readings is akin to the "vain repetition" that Jesus warned us about—so why are we putting out a book that apparently advocates the same?

Here's why: Many Christians say, "Just speak to God what's in your heart—you don't need the written prayers." That's quite true! However…where does that idea end? If we don't "need" prayers in a book, do we need hymnals? What about church buildings? And, you know, why do we get together for worship on Sunday? Can't we simply gather in the middle of the street whenever the spirit moves us? Sure we could! But we don't. The church buildings, the hymns, the prayers—they're all tools to help us better connect with God spiritually, mentally, emotionally, and even physically.

Getting even more practical, my friend Rachel can pray off the cuff better than anybody I know—but her husband, Frank, can't pray his way out of a paper bag. Both Rachel and Frank could use this book! Frank will feel more at ease praying because there's a guide—and the repeated words will soon feel like his own. Rachel could use this book merely as a jumping-off point. She could begin something like the Youth Worker's Prayer (page 108) and then launch into her own supplications when the time comes.

That's why we use liturgy.

Liturgy forges pathways to change.

Rick didn't want to come. His mother made him. Since their move, he hadn't wanted to go to church, but she dragged him along anyway. Rick started going to youth group meetings because of the girls. When the youth minister invited him to the winter retreat, he thought "Sure, why not?"

But now he was stuck. It was after 11 p.m., and the group was sitting in a circle while the youth minister read a prayer. Rick fiddled with the unlit candle in his hands. The room was dark. The youth minister was the only one with a lit candle, and he was using it to read.

"I want you to pray with me," the youth minister said. "When I say a phrase, I want you to respond with, 'God is beside us on the path.'" The leader read some things about getting lost and finding the way. Rick said the words out loud with the others. He noticed that by the end of the reading they had all seemed to match each other's tone

and inflection. Like a spoken chorus.

"Now," the leader said, "I want you to pray silently for someone else in the group. After your candle is lit, go and light that person's candle. I'll go first."

The youth minister sat there for a full minute with his eyes closed. Rick watched him. Then the leader stood up and walked across the circle to a kid who Rick had sat with at dinner. Rick didn't remember the kid's name. The youth minister lit the kid's candle and sat down again. The kid closed his eyes (his lips moved when he prayed). He seemed to hit the "amen" and then stood up. He walked over to the girl Rick sort of liked and lit her candle. (Rick had been hoping to do that.) She sat quietly for a while. Rick saw her eyes getting moist; she sniffed once and then wiped her eyes with her fingers. She walked over to Rick and passed on the light to him. He sat there stunned. She had prayed for him? (She did.) As far as he knew, no one had ever said a prayer just for him. He wasn't sure what to do. He bowed his head and at first thought of his mother, then of his dad who had left them, then he thought of Mitch, the guy he shot hoops with earlier in the day. "God, be with him on the path," he said to himself. It was all he could think of. Rick stood and lit Mitch's candle and sat back down. When everyone's candle had a light, the youth leader started to read a prayer. Rick listened this time. He had a strange feeling, like something was about to happen.

Liturgy builds community and creates embodied participation.

Nicole liked the services that Greg, the youth minister, planned. She always felt as though she was part of it. He used a lot of responsive readings. He often asked her to be one of the psalm readers or to read one of the prayers. She knew there were other girls who had better speaking voices, but Greg didn't seem to care about that...he just wanted everyone to be a part of the experience. When she worshiped with the youth group, she found she was listening to what was being said rather than listening for what was coming next. It was like she was listening with her whole body. In those services, she was really part of something.

A Change of Heart

There was a time I never would have purchased this book, let alone written it. But I had a change of heart, a conversion if you will, regarding liturgy. I believe that liturgy and ritual can do all of those things I've just shared. I've seen those things happen with my own eyes. Some instances I can explain. Others leave me with no more of an explanation than if you'd asked me about the movement of the Holy Spirit.

So any attempt on my part to demystify the use of liturgy may be a waste of time—but I will try.

Let's start with the gospel.

Every teacher who's been instructed in the kingdom of God is like the owner of a house who brings out of his storeroom new treasures as well as old. (Matthew 13:52)

Teenagers are gradually discovering liturgy as a treasure that possesses depth and richness. In other cases, it is an old and forgotten treasure that's been rediscovered.

For youth ministers, liturgy is worth bringing out of the storeroom—no matter what the denomination or tradition.

History

The book of Leviticus begins where the book of Exodus ends. God had delivered the people to the foot of Mount Sinai, and he was ready to teach the people how to worship.

A lot of ancient worship practices aren't part of our services these days. For instance, we no longer have animal sacrifices. (Now wouldn't that tick off the custodian?) We do, however, have liturgy and ritual at our disposal in our churches—practices that have been in existence for centuries.

The services in Leviticus were designed for the worshipers of their day. We have our own ways. Liturgy in worship is designed to help reveal a loving, powerful, and forgiving God. The prayers, readings, psalms, and services in this book are written to help youth workers focus the hearts of teenagers on God. They are written in common language that speaks and instructs new and young believers.

But make no mistake: *Liturgy does not take the place of a truly heart-centered relationship with God.*

We owe a great debt to the Church of England. It created many of what we call "modern" liturgies and emphasized the importance of ritual long before weary travelers landed on Plymouth Rock. When they arrived in the new world, they tossed out old ways and began to worship like jazz musicians blowing freeform. But eventually they found their worship lacking—and they slowly began bringing back the traditions that had connected them with God. They still amended them and shaped them over time, making them relevant to their cultural situation. And in the end, they opened a long-closed window and once again allowed the Holy Spirit to blow into their lives like a gentle breeze.

There is an incredible hunger among teenagers for deeper spirituality. Creeds, candles, silence, angels, and sacred practices are all gaining understanding and popularity. Teenagers are seeking things with a fragrance of the otherworldly or mysterious.

But in our efforts to attract the widest possible audience, many of us have unfortunately left behind a generation seeking depth and meaning in a connection with God.

This book contains all the treasures you need to construct new ways of connecting your students with the Creator, build community, and open that window for God to enter in and change their lives.

Daily Prayers

In this section are prayers you can repeat over and over as part of your daily prayer life. The words are meant to be a starting point for your private meditations. Read the words aloud each time you pray. Eventually they'll feel like your own.

Monday: A Prayer for Patience

FATHER, GOD, I begin this new day and this new week seeking your help.
When I lack energy, give me your spirit.
When I lack discipline, give me your love.
When I lack time, give me your patience.
I have much to do, God.
Smile on my tasks.

(Name urgent items on your to-do list.)

Help me to please all those I need to please.
…or at least help them be patient with me.
Let the patience and forgiveness I receive from others
equal the patience I extend to them.
The world around me seems to be spinning out of control.
I am worried about _____ *(think of places or people in the news).*
Be with us, Lord.
I go through this life as best I can
and sometimes it's just barely enough.
Other times I fall seriously short of the mark.
Walk with me.
Make me aware of your presence this week.
I will give you the glory.
Amen.

Tuesday: A Prayer for Faithfulness

I will not question you, God.
I will go where you send me.
I will deal with all that comes my way.
I will open my heart to you and
believe that all things will work out
for my good
because I love you.
I will listen to the Scriptures.
I will learn from them.
I will pray and know I am heard.
You, Lord, are not my destination on this journey.
Because you are beside me while I walk.
You, Lord, are the journey itself.

I am a servant of the Creator of the universe.
I will not be bogged down by _____ *(name things that are keeping you from focusing on your work for God).*
God will lift my spirit.
I will not be dragged into the muck and mire.
I am a servant of God.
Amen.

Wednesday: A Prayer for Kindness

God, there are times when I just want to throw someone through a wall.
And the week is barely half over!
Help me be kind to those who aren't.
Help me be kind to my family and friends who must live with me.
Help me to be kind to those who try the patience I prayed for on Monday.
I'm feeling overwhelmed, God.
Stand beside me.
Let me feel your presence.

(Take a moment and sit in silence. Breathe deeply. Calm yourself.)

Stay with me, God.
Get me through this crazy week.
Help me deal with these crazy people.
Fill my soul.
Amen.

Thursday: A Prayer for Peace

I am your servant, God.
When there is chaos around me, help me stay centered.
When those around me argue and fight,
let me be your peacemaker.
Show me what's important.
Help me to keep an open mind.
Help me soothe the anger of others.
Help me remember what is truly important.
Help me resolve the conflicts in my life.

*(Name aloud the chaotic situations and people with whom you're struggling;
include yourself and the tough decisions you must face.)*

Stay with me, God.
Enter into the hearts of all those
with whom I cannot find common ground.
Fill their hearts and fill mine.
Let us stop fussing and find peace.
I am your servant, God.
Amen.

Friday: A Prayer for Self-Control

God, I don't always live the way I should.
I tell the world about being honest and true and pure.
Then sometimes they look at me and run.
When I said I'd be your servant, I thought it would be easier.
I thought you'd take away all my problems and temptations.
I thought I could be the kind of person I tell others they should be.
It doesn't always work that way, God.
I see others having a wonderful time, and I miss being part of that.
I see something shiny off to the side of the path
and I go wandering after it without a thought.

*(Think of some temptations in your life; things that
distract your mind from God's will for you.)*

Keep my head right, God.
Keep my eyes focused on Jesus.
Keep my feet on the path.
Keep my heart desiring what is good.
Everything is permissible, but not everything is beneficial.
Help me know the difference.
And when I already know the difference
help me make the right choice anyway.
Amen.

Saturday: A Prayer of Joy

God, there is something about Saturday I love.
With childlike innocence I love this day.
Even if I'm working.
Even if I'm stuck doing something I'd rather not do.
I love this day.
My body and mind may have ideas for my time
but my heart wants to watch cartoons and eat sugarcoated cereal with ice-cold milk.
Thank you for all the wonderful things I never think to thank you for.
Thank you for children.
Thank you for cartoons.
Thank you for granulated sugar, cereal, and ice-cold milk.
Thank you for _____.

(Name aloud other little things for which you seldom thank God.)

God, waking up on a Saturday morning is like
waking up to a warm hug.
If I sweat this day in my backyard, I will thank you for the rain.
If I strain through this day shoveling snow, I will thank you for the sunshine.
My days on this earth are few compared to the eternity I want to spend with you, God.
May heaven be one big, long Saturday.
Amen.

Sunday: A Prayer of Love

This is your day, God.
I will use it to honor you.
I will stand here and inhale your air.
I will feel the sunlight on my face.
I will sing your songs.
I will praise your name.
I will remember you in all things, God.
When the sun goes down today,
I will remember you.
I will thank you for the gift of living another week.
(And thank you for getting me through the last one.)
Thank you for my family and my friends.
Thank you for your patience.
Thank you for the faith you put in me even when I let you down.
Thank you for your kindness.
Thank you for your peace that's beyond my understanding
Thank you for your self-control.
Thank you for the joy you've given me.
Thank you for your love, God.
I am your servant.
Amen.

Services

In this section you'll find worship experiences for special events such as Good Friday and Christmas, as well as reuseable services for lock-ins, retreats, and mission trips. Use these services as a "base" and then add your own prayers and readings, or choose something from the prayers and readings sections of the book.

A Service For All Hallows Eve

Style	Memorial, meditative, sorta creepy
Location	Cemetery or darkened sanctuary
Length	30 to 45 minutes
Materials	Bibles, boom box, candles, a thurible (a container for burning incense)
Scripture	1 Samuel 28:2-25; Job 4:12-21; Psalm 4, 23, 123; Ezekiel 37:1-14
Music Suggestions	"When All Is Said and Done" by Geoff Moore & the Distance, "Take Me to the River" sung by Annie Lennox (*Medusa* CD), soft jazz or light classical music
Comments/Ideas	If you have any sparklers left from the 4th of July, use them to illustrate how we often "burn brightly" and then "go out."

Introduction

Don't freak out. This really is a worship service for All Hallows Eve—and it's really cool.

Centuries ago, the early church noticed that the druids were worshiping in the cemetery on one specific night of the year. They weren't offering human sacrifices— they were burning dried crops to their gods in thanks for a plentiful harvest.

When the early church began to create its calendar in the 800s, it placed All Saints Day on the day following the druid festival. Churches began worshiping in the cemeteries on All Hallows Eve as part of the All Saints Day celebration. It was a somber service about death and life-after-death.

The order of worship here is based on a service from the *Episcopal Book of Occasional Services*. You can add communion to this service as an example of everlasting life or as a death-is-not-the-end theme.

I first did this service with a group of teenagers in 1996. We were in a cemetery in Akron, Ohio. My assistant at the time knew a monk from a monastery in Cleveland. We invited him to come along. The cemetery was very old. It had a lot of statues and not much light. We used the Annie Lennox version of "Take Me to the River" by the Talking Heads as a processional.

Brother Jacob brought a thurible (a swinging incense burner), and we walked through a cemetery and read Scripture about the dead coming to life.

This service is a wonderful way to bring some Halloween back to your church if you've had controversy in the past. It can also be used as a service in which your youth leads the congregation.

You can add music to this service wherever you feel it's appropriate. The best song I've ever used in the service is "When All Is Said and Done" by Geoff Moore & the Distance. It's an excellent closer.

Another cool idea is to have your psalm readers surrounding the congregation. Each reader takes one line of a psalm. This produces an "enclosed" sensation for those worshipping.

I've also used a variation of "The Shield of St. Patrick" as a closing prayer. It's very powerful, especially in the hands of a good reader. At the end of the service, invite those in attendance to stay as long as they'd like. When they're ready, have them blow out the candles and leave quietly.

Order of Worship

Opening Prayer

God, we gather in this place on this night to remember. We remember the words of your son when he said, "I am the resurrection and the life. If you believe in me, you will never die but have eternal life." Many of us have had someone close to us go home to be with you, God. We are selfish to want them here with us instead of with you. Watch over us here, God. It's only a matter of time before we're all together again in your arms. Guide us now as we come into your presence. *Amen.*

Scripture

Job 4:12-21

Reading

Psalm 4

interpreted

God, you are my guardian.
Listen to me again, God.
I've been in this spot before, and you helped me.
God, we chase after stupid things.
We fill our lives with worthless possessions
Because we don't know what's really important.
God, as we lay quietly in our beds searching our souls
Let us remember that we owe you—and not the other way around.
There are blessings all around us, Lord.
You give us all that we need.
We can lie down and sleep soundly.
We have no worries.
You will always be there to protect us.
Amen.

Scripture

1 Samuel 28:3-25. *For this passage, assign the reading in parts and read the Scripture as if it were a script. You will need a narrator, Saul, Samuel, and a witch.*

Reading

Psalm 23

interpreted

I am not alone.
God will lead me.
God will let me rest beside the water.
God will let me regain my strength.
It's a dark world.
It's full of scary people.
God is with me.
The Lord is with me.

The creator of the universe is by my side.

Nothing can harm me.

God plans a party for me

And all those who laughed at me will have to stand outside and watch.

My glass will never be empty.

God is with me every move that I make.

I will live in God's house forever.

Amen.

Lighting Candles

Instruct that the candle lighting is to be done in silence. Ask each participant to think about a departed loved one. You can send "lighters" into the congregation, or you can start one flame and allow it to be passed along until everyone has a light.

Scripture

Ezekiel 37:1-14

Reading

Psalm 143

interpreted

Hear me God

Hear my cries of for relief

Save me.

Don't judge me, Lord. Nobody is perfect.

There are those who wait for me.

They make me feel like I'm already in my coffin.

My soul is weak

My heart is confused.

I read your Word

I see your creation

I am praying to you like a desert prays for rain.

Answer me, God.

Don't leave me down in this hole.

Let hope come with the rising of the sun.

You are my guide.

Show me the way.

I will trust you.

Silence my enemies.

I will give you my soul.

Destroy my foes.

I am your servant.

Closing Prayer

I bind to myself today

The virtue of love,
In the obedience of angels,
In the hope of resurrection
In prayers of patriarchs,
In predictions of prophets,
In preaching of apostles,
In faith of confessors.

I bind to myself today
The power of heaven,
The light of the sun,
The brightness of the moon,
The splendor of fire,
The flashing of lightning,
The swiftness of wind,
The depth of sea,
The stability of earth,
The density of rocks.

I bind to myself today
God's power to guide me,
God's might to uphold me,
God's wisdom to teach me,
God's eye to watch over me,
God's ear to hear me,
God's word to give me speech,
God's hand to guide me,
God's way to lie before me,
God's shield to shelter me,
God's host to secure me,

Christ with me, Christ before me,
Christ behind me, Christ within me,
Christ beneath me, Christ above me,
Christ at my right, Christ at my left,
Christ in the heart of everyone who thinks of me,
Christ in the mouth of everyone who speaks to me,
Christ in every eye that sees me,
Christ in every ear that hears me.

I bind to myself today
The strong virtue of Christ,
I believe the Trinity in the unity of the creator of the universe.

Closing Song

"When All Is Said and Done" by Geoff Moore & the Distance

Services for Communion

Style	Formal or serious or meditative
Location	Outdoors or in a sanctuary
Length	30 minutes
Materials	Bread, juice, boom box, Bibles
Scripture	Psalm 63, Luke 22:7-20, 1 Corinthians 3:15-17, Colossians 3:12-17
Music Suggestions	Tracks 1, 6, 8, or 9 from the *Eucharist* CD in the back of this book.
Comments/Ideas	You can have the youth make their own bread as part of the service. A simple mixture of wheat flour and water is enough for the kind of unleavened bread eaten in Jesus' time. If someone in your group has an automatic bread machine, set it to finish just before the service begins. The smell of fresh bread adds a nice quality to the service.
	Also, never underestimate the power of candles!

Snacks at the Altar?

I grew up in a small Methodist church. Once a month or so, we had a communion service during which the congregants came forward, kneeled at the altar, and received a small cube of white bread and a small paper cup of grape juice. As a little kid, I remember thinking of it as a "snack" that the grown-ups got to have. I didn't take communion until after I was confirmed.

I went to work for the Episcopal Church about 10 years ago. There I began to discover and study the amazing holiness that permeates the communion service. Regardless of your denomination, there is a basic holiness accompanying it. One of the first Eucharist services with which I helped was outdoors at a camp. The priest asked for my help and held the chalice filled with wine. After the teens had all been to the table, the priest pointed to the cup and said, "You have to finish that." I was never a drinker, yet here I stood with wine in my hands. (Yes, I finished it. To throw it away would have been unthinkable. It was a long way from the "communion snack" I observed as a child.)

Communion (also known as the Eucharist, the Lord's Table, Celebration of the Lord's Supper, and by other names) is the recreation of the final Passover meal that Christ celebrated with his followers.

What communion truly means is a matter of faith, not opinion. There are those who

believe that, with the blessing, the elements become the actual body and blood of Jesus. They believe a holy "transubstantiation" occurs, and the act of communion becomes more than symbolic.

Others believe the entire process is purely symbolic. That eating "Wonder Bread and Welch's" is simply a vehicle by which to honor Christ by doing what he asked—to remember him.

I'm in no way attempting to offer the definitive definition of communion. I'm not saying what is right or wrong as we celebrate the Last Supper. It's a matter of faith. We leave the meaning up to you and your teenagers. All we're doing here is presenting two communion services. One is a celebration that includes dance and joyful noise. The other is a quiet, meditative service that works best with small groups in intimate settings.

One thing is certain about communion, however: It's an important service! Whatever your denomination believes or supports with regard to bread and juice, most agree that Jesus said, "Do this in remembrance of me." It's one of the few liturgical directions that Christ gave us. Communion is practiced in the cathedrals of Rome and in the smallest community churches in rural Iowa.

It is, therefore, an important service to explore with your students.

A Service for Communion (Version 1)

Version 1 is an upbeat communion service. It can include dance as well as active participation by the congregation. For Version 1, it's necessary to use the *Eucharist* CD in the back of the book as a guide for the communion service. The entire service can be completed standing up.

Allow your group to dance "as the spirit moves them" if you use track 1 as an opener.

You can also use track 6 as opening music, but a certain amount of response is necessary. In this case, you can print the responses on poster board and hang them at the front of the room. You can also make up simple hand motions for the responses. Demonstrate these before the service. If you have dancers in your group, play them the CD and ask them to come up with the hand motions.

The Service

Opening

Option 1: God is here. Let us give thanks to God. *Amen.*

Option 2: Father, Son, and Holy Spirit, come into our hearts and minds. Lift us and bring us into your presence. *Amen.*

Music

Use track 1 or track 6 from the Eucharist *CD from the back of the book.*

A Prayer of Confession

*Instruct your group to reply, "**Forgive us, God**" after each leader statement. If possible, have your group circle up and hold hands as the prayer is read.*

Leader: For all hurtful things we have said to each other

Group: Forgive us God

Leader: For all the things we should have said but didn't

Group: Forgive us God

Leader: For ignoring the lonely

Group: Forgive us God

Leader: For changing ourselves just to be popular

Group: Forgive us God

Leader: For going along with the crowd

Group: Forgive us God

Leader: For listening to those who didn't have our best interests at heart

Group: Forgive us God

Leader: For ignoring you

Group: Forgive us God

Leader: For asking you for worthless things

Group: Forgive us God

Leader: For wanting what we don't need

Group: Forgive us God

Leader: For taking what we don't want

Group: Forgive us God

Leader: For taking for granted all the good gifts you give us

Group: Forgive us God

Leader: For believing we are alone

Group: Forgive us God

Leader: We believe in a God of second chances. We rely on the forgiveness and grace promised us by Jesus. May we come to the table of Christ as new creations. May we sit at the table as forgiven people. *Amen.*

Scripture

Colossians 3:12-17 or 1 Corinthians 3:15-17

Psalm 16

interpreted

When my life gets tough, I will turn to God.

I will say to God, "You are my shelter. Without you, nothing I do matters."

I will follow those who have chosen to follow God.

I will ignore those who follow other gods.

God is my food.

God is my drink.

God speaks to me in my dreams.

God speaks to me in my heart.

God is all around me.

In God my heart is glad.

My soul rejoices.

My body rests.

I will follow the path of God and find fullness and joy in my life.

Amen.

Music

Play track 9 from the Eucharist *CD from the back of the book.*

Prepare the communion table during this song. Pass out the bread and the cup and instruct everyone to hold the elements until the CD instructs them to "eat" and "drink."

Final Prayer

Creator God, we take the body and blood of your son into our bodies. Let Jesus be a part of us as you are a part of him. Guide our hearts and thoughts and allow us to be one in the body of Christ. May Christ be part of all we think about and do. May his body and blood nourish and make us whole. *Amen.*

Closing/Benediction

Father, Son, and Holy Spirit, go with us now as we go back into the world. Help us create a world worthy of your continued presence. *Amen.*

A Service for Communion (Version 2)

Version 2 is more meditative than version 1. This communion service works best with groups of 20 or less and makes more use of silence and prayer. (Optional: Use the Eucharist CD's track 8, "Prayer," as background music.) You'll need one candle for each person the group or one for the center of the circle. This is a great service to do outdoors in the evening.

The Service

Opening

Option 1: God, come into this quiet place. Surround us and hold us. Be in our hearts and minds as we enter into this time of communion. *Amen.*

Option 2: Creator, stay beside us, above us, and beneath us. Watch over us this quiet night as we hear your Word and taste the bread and the cup. Enter into us, God. *Amen.*

Psalm 63

interpreted

The tradition of the Passover meal includes singing a song—we assume Jesus and his disciples did the same at the Last Supper.

We seek you, God.
We have waiting hearts for you.
Like dry summer grass longs for a slow drenching rain
We wait for you.
We have seen the miracles.
We have felt your presence in the sanctuary and in holy places.
We long to feel your presence in this place now.
We will pray to you until the day we die.
We would give up all that we have to feel your arms around us.
A moment with you is like being invited to the party of the year.
As we lie awake in bed, we will listen for you.
We will sing songs about you in the night.
Those that mock you and laugh at me for believing in you
Eventually will be cold and silent.
Your kingdom is where the party is.
We will dance and sing and celebrate for eternity.
Amen.

Confession in Silence

Instruct your group to meditate silently on the things in their weeks or in their lives that they've done wrong. Have them offer up these things up to God in the quiet of their own minds. During this time play track 8 from the Eucharist CD. This four-minute track creates a nice, quiet mood for the rest of the service. Place a variety of candles on the table. As students feel they have "given something to God," have them stand and light any of the candles. When the students have returned to their seats, allow the track to finish, and then continue.

Assurance

Leader: God, we often fall short of the mark. Then again, you never said this path was an easy one. We carry such heavy baggage with us. We ask that you help us leave behind the things we don't need. We also ask that you help us carry the things we can't give up yet. We know someday we'll come to you free of all the things that hold us back or drag us down. Until then walk with us, God. We give all these things to you. *Amen.*

Scripture

Read Luke 22:7-20

If possible have an assistant "prepare the table" while the Scripture is read. If you're leading this service on your own, prepare the table in silence and then read the Scripture. You can use the interpreted text below, or you can use the Scripture passage.

The rain had cooled things off. The day had been hot and dry, but the brief rain made the evening comfortable. A cool breeze came through the window, and Jesus tilted his head back, feeling the air on his hot skin. He smelled the night. He could smell the sea. He wanted to take one last look at the beach before he had to go, but there wasn't time.

The room was prepared just as he said it would be. Jesus wasn't surprised—for him it was the same as breathing. It wasn't something you had to remind yourself to do. It just happened. He did, however, still enjoy seeing the look on Peter's face when things like that happened. Peter, his most trusted disciple—the only one who actually stepped out of the boat—was still surprised at the power. He still didn't get it. None of them did really. Though they understood more than most. But in a few hours, Jesus' best friend would turn him over to his enemies, and his most loyal pupil would deny him.

Jesus wanted to make this moment last. He wanted to give them all something they could keep forever. The Passover celebration was winding down. His friends were still laughing and lounging on the pillows the servants had placed on the floor. Jesus saw the bread and the cup on the table.

He asked them all to gather around. They scooted in toward him and grew quiet. (Judas was on the end. He was the only one who didn't smile during the Passover celebration. He'd barely spoken a word.) Jesus looked around the table. He met the eyes of each of these men...these true friends. They had spent the last three years together, and most of them still didn't realize the end was near—or maybe that the real beginning was near. Jesus smiled at the paradox. The disciples smiled, too, but they didn't know why. They were happy just to see him smile. He hadn't smiled much lately.

Jesus picked up one of the loaves of bread that had not been eaten, and he broke it in half. Handing half to Peter on his left and the other half to John on his right, he said, "Take some and eat it. This is my body."

They all took some. Jesus picked up the cup of wine. He swirled the dark liquid in the cup and stared at it for a moment. Then he passed it to Peter. "Everyone drink some. This is my blood. It is the sign of the promise." Jesus smiled inwardly at that. They would debate that one for years.

Play track 10 from the Eucharist *CD as you begin serving communion. This track is less than four minutes long. You may want to have other music ready or have an assistant ready to hit the repeat button until everyone has been served.*

A Prayer of Thanksgiving (Responsive Reading)

Instruct your group to quietly reply, "We will listen for God," after each leader statement.

Leader: In the quiet of the night
Group: We will listen for God.
Leader: In the silence of the moment
Group: We will listen for God.
Leader: Like Elijah who listened after the hurricane
Group: We will listen for God.
Leader: Like David on the roof of the palace
Group: We will listen for God.
Leader: Like Samuel lying awake in bed.
Group: We will listen for God.
Leader: Now and tomorrow
Group: We will listen for God.
Leader: When we laugh, and when we pray
Group: We will listen for God.
Leader: When we hear music or the tears of children
Group: We will listen for God.
Leader: When we need to give advice to a friend
Group: We will listen for God.
Leader: When our own words are not enough
Group: We will listen for God.
Leader: When our own lives are in trouble.
Group: We will listen for God.
Leader: When there is no one else to turn to
Group: We will listen for God.
Leader: *Amen.*

Blessing

Go now. You are part of Jesus, and Jesus is part of you. *Amen.*

A "Dumpster" Christmas Service

Style	Experiential
Location	Outside (if possible, hold the service behind a hotel next to a dumpster)
Length	30 minutes.
Materials	Bible, boom box, candles and matches, a flashlight
Scripture	Isaiah 9:2-7; Luke 1:26-2:21; Philippians 2:5-8
Music Suggestions	"Kyrie," track 5 from the enclosed *Eucharist* CD, "Gabriel's Message" performed by Sting on the *Very Special Christmas* CD. (This is a great service for live music. "O Little Town of Bethlehem," for instance, takes on new meaning when you're standing behind a hotel in the cold.)
Comments/Ideas	The less your students know about this service, the better.

Introduction

This is a very cool, experiential service that takes some preplanning but can work really well.

Imagine your students showing up to a meeting one Sunday night before Christmas. They are immediately loaded into cars and driven into the city. You park in a parking lot and begin to walk (even if it's raining or snowing). You walk to the nearest hotel and bring the whole group into the lobby. Everyone hears you ask for a room. The clerk replies, "Sorry, there is no room here." As you turn to leave, the clerk adds, "We do have a dumpster out back if you'd like to use that." Take your group around to the dumpster and hold a worship service next to it that talks about a teenage couple, cold and alone, having a baby right where they're standing.

A few days before the service, visit one or two of the hotels in your area. Speak with the manager and tell him or her that you want to hold a worship service by the dumpster. If the manager says, "No," thank him or her and try someplace else.

I did this service once, and the manager thought the idea was so cool that he put up a tarp beside the dumpster. It was rank. The tarp leaked and we worshipped God with a steady stream of cold rain dripping through the middle of our worship area. It was perfect.

Order of Worship

Opening/Invocation

Option 1: Make your word known to our hearts, God. Help us to know your Son. *Amen.*

Option 2: We enter into a time of hope, faith, peace, and love. Be with us on the journey, God. *Amen.*

Prayer

Option 1: God, it's cold and wet, and we are uncomfortable. We can only begin to imagine what it was like for two scared teenagers who left all they had to follow a vision. Give us the faith of Mary who said, "Yes," and made the greatest commitment anyone was ever asked to make. Give us the faith of Joseph who faced public ridicule and stood by the woman he loved because of his faith in you. Give us faith like that, God. *Amen.*

Option 2: God, tonight we will go back to our warm homes. But Mary and Joseph had no place to go. Their lives were changing forever on this night, and they entered into this responsibility willingly—and without a clue. They had faith, hope, love, and the word of an angel to guide them. Help us to follow that path tonight, God. Let us seek the faith, hold on to the hope, express that love, and listen for that angel's voice to guide us. *Amen.*

Music

Choose an appropriate piece here or use track 5, "Kyrie," on the Eucharist *CD.*

Responsive Reading

Instruct your group to quietly reply, "He was born in a stable," after each leader statement.

Leader: Jesus wasn't born in a hospital with modern equipment.

Group: He was born in a stable.

Leader: He wasn't born in the comfortable hotel inn with hundreds of people attending his every need.

Group: He was born in a stable.

Leader: Jesus wasn't born into kingly privilege, although God could have made that happen.

Group: He was born in a stable.

Leader: Jesus was born to teenage parents.

Group: He was born in a stable.

Leader: In a small town.

Group: He was born in a stable.

Leader: Behind a hotel.

Group: He was born in a stable.

Leader: He was the Son of God, coming into the world as a common man.

Group: He was born in a stable.

Leader: Working as a carpenter, like his father.

Group: He was born in a stable.

Leader: His voice was like a common man's.

Group: He was born in a stable.

Leader: But his teachings were of God.

Group: He was born in a stable.

Leader: He came into this world for us.

Group: He was born in a stable.

Leader: So that we could understand him.

Group: He was born in a stable.

Leader: So that we would learn his lessons.

Group: He was born in a stable.

Leader: So that we could be saved.

Group: He was born in a stable.

Leader: We are grateful.

Group: He was born in a stable.

Leader: *Amen.*

Psalm 89

God, I will sing your songs forever.

I will sing them to the world.

Those generations yet to be born will hear my songs

God said to David, "From your house I will bring the savior of the world."

Our God is the most powerful.

Our God is the creator of the universe.

Our God can call forth the storms or calm them.

Our God can shape the mountains or bring them down.

The world and all its people belong to you, God.

God, bless all those who join in this celebration.

We sing and dance all day.

Your kindness gives us strength.

David was chosen to be King.

God promised the house of David would last until the last star fell from the sky.

Amen.

Scripture

Old Testament Isaiah 9:2-7; New Testament Philippians 2:5-8

Candles

Pass out and light candles, one for each member of your group.

The Christmas Story

This is one of the most beautiful stories ever told. If you can, have someone tell the story rather than read it. If you are not comfortable as a storyteller, you'll find the passage in **Luke 1:26 -2:21**.

Closing/Benediction

Option 1: On a night like this, more than two thousand years ago, the world was changed forever. May our hearts be changed, and may we never be the same from this moment forward. *Amen.*

Option 2: God you sent your son to earth to teach us all about love. May we learn the lessons and may we, with Jesus' help, live by them forever. *Amen.*

Music

Choose an appropriate piece of music to send the group on its way.

A Service For Good Friday

Style	Reflective, serious, experiential
Location	Sanctuary
Length	about an hour
Materials	A six-foot wooden cross, candles, 30 quarters, nails, two large crescent wrenches, matches
Scripture	Psalm 22, 40, 69, 109; Luke 23:33-46
Music Suggestions	*The Prayer Cycle* (wonderful, moody music), "Fragile" from Sting's *Nothing Like the Sun* CD (a moving piece that can sound like the words of Christ in the garden), "Jesus, He Loves Me" by Edwin McCain from the *Jesus Movie* soundtrack.
Comments/Ideas	Lots of work but well worth the effort.

Introduction

For the most part, church people are happy people. In the spring, our attentions turn to Easter. Easter (along with Christmas) is our big time of year. We buy new clothes and lots of chocolate and spend days coloring eggs. Easter is the celebration of life, new birth, vibrant colors, and music that makes the windows rattle.

But can we truly celebrate the resurrection of our Savior if we don't fully remember his death? Many churches skip Good Friday altogether. "Too depressing. Nobody comes," they say. Instead, our Wednesday Night Lenten Dinners are lighthearted discussions with motivational speakers.

Where is the darkness? If Easter is the light, then isn't there darkness connected to it?

If Easter makes you want to sing and jump for joy and celebrate, then Good Friday should make you want to crawl into a corner and weep.

What follows is a service for Good Friday. There are many options available. What you use depends on what resources you have. We've presented various ideas here, along with the basic order of worship.

Your first decision is whether you want to lead this service for your youth or have your youth lead the service for the entire congregation. It's a wonderful opportunity to get the youth involved in Holy Week. (Other than when they get "volunteered" to clean up after various functions.)

Here are some ideas:

Darkness. A powerful worship tool. Prior to the service, leave on just enough light for people to find their seats, then take the lights out completely. Leave the lights out for the entire service.

Cross of Candles. *Option 1.* Have an adult volunteer build you a six- to eight-foot cross. It should stand on its own yet have a removable base. Place five candles on the cross—two where Jesus' hands were, one where his head was, and one where his feet were. Finally place one in the center. Paint the whole thing black. As the service progresses and the Scriptures are read, blow out the candles one at a time. As Christ gets closer to death, the cross will get darker. When the Scripture, "With this he breathed his last," is read, blow out the center candle.

It's a nice touch to have worship leaders (youth or adults) remove the cross from its base and carry it from the sanctuary on their shoulders like a coffin. Find an appropriate piece of music to accompany this.

Option 2. If your church has a balcony, you can create a cross by placing boards on the backs of the pews on the floor. Place a candle on each board. From the floor, the cross isn't visible, but once you get to the balcony and look down, then you can see it. Use the same process of blowing out candles as Jesus gets closer to death.

Psalms. You can create a creepy special effect (and a cheap one, too) by reading the psalms in the following way:

Choose four to six readers (preferably all one gender) and give them the psalms. Have them practice reading the psalms simultaneously. Try to get them to match tone and inflection so they sound like one voice. Then place them at each corner of the sanctuary. Space the others along the sides or in the balcony.

As they begin reading, switch things up by having each reader start one line later than the last reader. The result is an echo effect that makes you feel surrounded, and the mood it creates is almost claustrophobic. At first you can't understand what's being said, but soon the brain adjusts and the words to the psalm become understandable. And there is no way to tune it out.

Cruuusssssssifyyyy. During the "Pilate" reading, it's very effective to have the reader act angry. Have the reader actually yell at the congregation as if it is the angry crowd. Put the rest of your team at the back of the church and instruct them to (very quietly) all whisper the word "crucify"—even have them stretch it out with a snakelike hiss: *Cruuussssssiifyyyy*. Let them stagger the word so each team member is starting and stopping the word differently than the others. As "Pilate" gets angrier, let the whispers get louder. Never bring it up to a speaking voice, though. Let the whisper get louder and louder. Sitting in the dark and hearing this "hiss" is extremely effective.

Thirty Pieces of Silver. Imagine a reading of the Scripture where Judas goes to Caiaphas and asks, "What will you give me if I betray him to you?" Caiaphas' answer can be followed by the sound of thirty pieces of silver (quarters). Drop these slowly onto a metal plate. Place the plate somewhere where the congregation can't see it. Put a microphone next to the plate for maximum effect.

The Hammer. Nothing brings it home like the sound of a hammer pounding in the nails. This can be extremely disconcerting for some. If you use this effect, you may want arrange for childcare if the youth are leading this service for the congregation. Over the years, we've found that the most effective sound is not a hammer on a nail—the best sound is achieved when you strike two large crescent wrenches together.

What Conclusion? Good Friday isn't the end of the story. Why end it? Yes, it's over, but there's more to come. Allow the service to simply end. As the last reader finishes the Scripture, have him or her blow out the last candle and walk out. Have your other worship leaders follow with the now darkened cross. Offer no closing prayer. Offer no word of hope. Let the congregation sit in the dark for a full minute and then slowly bring up the lights so they have just enough light to leave.

If you're allowed to have your youth lead the service for the congregation, ask your students to hide in the youth room or someplace else when the service is over. This was a service, not a performance. Your kids standing at the back of the church and shaking hands with the rest of the congregation will give them some affirmation, but it will dull the effect of the service on those in attendance.

Order of Worship

Music

Scripture

Psalm 40:11-14, 17

Do not withhold your mercy from me, O Lord;
may your love and your truth always protect me.
For troubles without number surround me;
my sins have overtaken me, and I cannot see.
They are more than the hairs of my head,
and my heart fails within me.

Be pleased, O Lord, to save me;
O Lord, come quickly to help me.
May all who seek to take my life
be put to shame and confusion;
may all who desire my ruin
be turned back in disgrace.
Yet I am poor and needy;
may the Lord think of me.
You are my help and my deliverer;
O my God, do not delay.

{ 34 }

Reading 1: Judas

The pain didn't stop. No matter what he did, Judas could barely lift himself off the ground. It was as if a tremendous weight was sitting on his chest. He felt like he could barely breathe. He leaned against the door of the house of Caiaphas; his hands felt like they weighed a hundred pounds each. When he knocked on the door, the ache from his knuckles passed through his body, and he nearly collapsed. The door opened, and Judas could tell by the way the servant stared at him that he must have looked as bad as he felt. Judas was led through a hall. The servant constantly had to stop and wait for Judas to catch up. The servant took him into a room where the chief priests sat on the floor around a table. Judas didn't even recognize the voice that came out of his own mouth:

"What will you give me if I bring Jesus to you?"

They whispered to each other. It didn't take them a full minute. The oldest of the priests stood and counted out 30 pieces of silver into Judas' hands. In spite of the cold he felt on his skin, the coins were so hot he thought surely they would brand his palms. When he stepped into the night, he took a deep breath and filled his lungs with air. It was the first deep breath he'd taken since he'd made his decision. He stood erect, and the pain in his chest and bones was gone. The throbbing in his head and subsided. But the coins still felt hot in his hand. He dumped them into a small leather pouch and tied it to his belt. He couldn't help hearing the coins jingle when he started walking down the dark road. It was an annoyance at first, but soon he was able to ignore it.

Candle is extinguished

Scripture

Psalm 69

Save me, O God,
for the waters have come up to my neck.
I sink in the miry depths,
where there is no foothold.
I have come into the deep waters;
the floods engulf me.
I am worn out calling for help;
my throat is parched.
My eyes fail, looking for my God.
Those who hate me without reason
outnumber the hairs of my head;
many are my enemies without cause,
those who seek to destroy me.
I am forced to restore
what I did not steal.

But I pray to you, O Lord,
in the time of your favor;
in your great love, O God,
answer me with your sure salvation.
Rescue me from the mire,
do not let me sink;
deliver me from those who hate me,
from the deep waters.
Do not let the floodwaters engulf me
or the depths swallow me up
or the pit close its mouth over me.
Answer me, O Lord, out of the goodness of your love;
in your great mercy turn to me.
Do not hide your face from your servant;
answer me quickly, for I am in trouble.
Come near and rescue me;
redeem me because of my foes.

You know how I am scorned, disgraced and shamed;
all my enemies are before you.
Scorn has broken my heart
and has left me helpless;
I looked for sympathy, but there was none,
for comforters, but I found none.
They put gall in my food
and gave me vinegar for my thirst.

Reading 2: Peter

Peter was the one they called "the rock." He was the strong one. He was the one who all the others leaned on when they began to question their beliefs. But on this night, when Jesus put his hands on Peter's shoulders, there was pain in the Messiah's eyes. He was hurt. His face had become heavy and no longer looked he'd be able to smile again. "Peter," he said, "tonight you will deny three times that you even know me." Peter's first response was that of disbelief. He knew there was no way he would deny his friend! But then he saw the Savior's eyes. He knew it was true. He knew. Peter's face then looked determined. He would prove him wrong! He would hide! He would go someplace where there were no people! He couldn't betray someone if there was no one to talk to, right? *Right?*

Candle is extinguished

Scripture

Psalm 109:1-31

O God, whom I praise,
do not remain silent,
for wicked and deceitful men
have opened their mouths against me;
they have spoken against me with lying tongues.
With words of hatred they surround me;
they attack me without cause.
In return for my friendship they accuse me,
but I am a man of prayer.
They repay me evil for good,
and hatred for my friendship.

But you, O Sovereign Lord,
deal well with me for your name's sake;
out of the goodness of your love, deliver me.
For I am poor and needy,
and my heart is wounded within me.
I fade away like an evening shadow;
I am shaken off like a locust.
My knees give way from fasting;
my body is thin and gaunt.
I am an object of scorn to my accusers;
when they see me, they shake their heads.

Help me, O Lord my God;
save me in accordance with your love.
Let them know that it is your hand,
that you, O Lord, have done it.
They may curse, but you will bless;
when they attack they will be put to shame,
but your servant will rejoice.
My accusers will be clothed with disgrace

and wrapped in shame as in a cloak.

With my mouth I will greatly extol the Lord;
in the great throng I will praise him.
For he stands at the right hand of the needy one,
to save his life from those who condemn him.

Reading 3: The Garden

In the garden, Jesus told his friends to sit and wait for him while he prayed. He walked just a few yards away before falling to his knees. He leaned against a large stone and pressed his tired face on the surface. The night air had become cool—and so was the stone. The sweat on his face and his hands began to chill him. Finally Jesus lifted himself on his knees and pressed his hands together so tightly that his knuckles turned white.

"Father," he said, "if it is possible, I don't want to die this way. But if you want me to...I will."

Jesus closed his eyes. He prayed so hard that blood began to seep from the pores of his skin and fall to the ground like thick clots of mud.

Music

"Fragile"

Candle is extinguished

Reading 4: Pilate

Scripture Reader: **John 19:10-12**

"Do you refuse to speak to me?" Pilate asked. "Don't you realize I have power either to free you or to crucify you?"

Jesus answered, "You would have no power over me if it were not given to you from above. Therefore the one who handed me over to you is guilty of a greater sin."

From then on, Pilate tried to set Jesus free, but the Jews kept shouting, "If you let this man go, you are no friend of Caesar. Anyone who claims to be a king opposes Caesar."

Pilate: What is it this man did to you?
Crowd: Cruuusssssiifyyyy
Pilate: I have found him guilty of nothing.
Crowd: Cruuusssssiifyyyy
Pilate: He is not a revolutionary.
Crowd: Cruuusssssiifyyyy
Pilate: He is no prophet.
Crowd: Cruuusssssiifyyyy
Pilate: He is a danger to no one.
Crowd: Cruuusssssiifyyyy
Pilate: I have given you Barabbas.
Crowd: Cruuusssssiifyyyy
Pilate: What has this man done?
Crowd: Cruuusssssiifyyyy

Pilate: I will whip him! Will that satisfy you?

Crowd: Cruuussssssiifyyyy

Pilate: But what has he done?

Crowd: Cruuussssssiifyyyy

Pilate: There is no need to crucify him!

Crowd: Cruuussssssiifyyyy

Pilate: What has he done?!?

Crowd: Cruuussssssiifyyyy

Pilate: Fine! He is yours!

Crowd: Cruuussssssiifyyyy

Pilate: I wash my hands of his blood!

Crowd: Cruuussssssiifyyyy

Pilate: This not my doing! You will take responsibility for his death!

The word "cruuussssssiifyyyy" continues and slowly begins fading out.

Sound Effect

Hammer

Candle is extinguished

Scripture

Psalm 22

My God, my God, why have you forsaken me?

Why are you so far from saving me,

so far from the words of my groaning?

O my God, I cry out by day, but you do not answer,

by night, and am not silent.

Yet you are enthroned as the Holy One;

you are the praise of Israel.

In you our fathers put their trust;

they trusted and you delivered them.

They cried to you and were saved;

in you they trusted and were not disappointed.

But I am a worm and not a man,

scorned by men and despised by the people.

All who see me mock me;

they hurl insults, shaking their heads:

"He trusts in the Lord;

let the Lord rescue him.

Let him deliver him,

since he delights in him."

Many bulls surround me;

strong bulls of Bashan encircle me.

Roaring lions tearing their prey
open their mouths wide against me.
I am poured out like water,
and all my bones are out of joint.
My heart has turned to wax;
it has melted away within me.
My strength is dried up like a potsherd,
and my tongue sticks to the roof of my mouth;
you lay me in the dust of death.
Dogs have surrounded me;
a band of evil men has encircled me,
they have pierced my hands and my feet.
I can count all my bones;
people stare and gloat over me.
They divide my garments among them
and cast lots for my clothing.

Scripture

Luke 23:33-46 *"Into your hands…"*

Play an appropriate piece of music and carry the cross out.

A Service For Sunrise

Style	Informal, meditative, quiet
Location	Hillside, dock near the water, rooftop
Length	20 minutes.
Materials	Bible, boom box
Scripture	Genesis 1, Psalm 19, Psalm 148
Music Suggestions	Soft. Light classical (possibly some Aaron Copeland). Track 8 from the *Eucharist* CD also works nicely.
Comments/Ideas	Keep it simple.

Introduction

Sunrise services are very popular in the planning stages, but when it comes to actually getting up in the morning to watch the sunrise, you may find yourself with a smaller attendance.

Still, it's possible to pull off both a sunrise service (for your chipper kids) and a morning service (for the full group). The Service for Morning is designed to get the blood pumping and the eyes open. But the Service for Sunrise is much quieter and creates a more contemplative mood. It's also quite short.

Plan a spot to meet prior to sunrise. (Check your local news for this info.) Needless to say the service should be outside. Find a spot on a hill, beside a lake, or on the roof. Don't ask the students to stand unless they want to. If you're on a retreat, they'll probably show up bleary-eyed and wrapped in their blankets. This is perfectly okay.

Order of Worship

Opening/Invocation

Option 1: The sun rises and the sky greets the light with colors and quiet. Let us begin this day with a clean heart. *Amen.*

Option 2: Creator God, you turn this planet around silently in space. Let the quiet of creation fill our minds and hearts. *Amen.*

Opening Prayer

Choose an appropriate sunrise prayer from the Prayers section of this book.

Responsive Reading

Use the following, instructing your group to reply with, "Remove the darkness, God" after the leader reads each line. Or you can choose a selection from the Responsive Readings section of this book.

Leader: The light begins slowly.

Group: Remove the darkness, God.

Leader: We couldn't take it all in one burst.

Group: Remove the darkness, God.

Leader: It would be too bright.

Group: Remove the darkness, God.

Leader: Our minds wouldn't grasp it.

Group: Remove the darkness, God.

Leader: In the same way God reveals himself to us.

Group: Remove the darkness, God.

Leader: We can't see God in all of his glory.

Group: Remove the darkness, God.

Leader: It would send us over the edge.

Group: Remove the darkness, God.

Leader: Slower is better.

Group: Remove the darkness, God.

Leader: We see things as we need to see them.

Group: Remove the darkness, God.

Leader: We learn things as we need to learn them.

Group: Remove the darkness, God.

Leader: All things happen in God's time, not ours.

Group: Remove the darkness, God.

Leader: The problems we face have answers.

Group: Remove the darkness, God.

Leader: The more we pay attention, the more we see.

Group: Remove the darkness, God.

Leader: The more we see, the more we understand.

Group: Remove the darkness, God.

Leader: God gave us the light as a gift.

Group: Remove the darkness, God.

Leader: We will follow the light.

Group: Remove the darkness, God.

Leader: His Word is a light on the dark path.

Group: Remove the darkness, God.

Leader: The light begins slowly.

Group: Remove the darkness, God.

Leader: We couldn't take it all in one burst.

Group: Remove the darkness, God.

Leader: *Amen.*

Psalm 148

Use the following "creation psalm." The writer of this psalm recognized that we don't know nearly as much as the angels, yet they praise God all day—should we do any less? One person can read this psalm, in order to avoid a group reading by those who've barely opened their eyes. The following psalm is the traditional NIV version. (Other suitable psalms for this service are Psalm 8, 51, 119, 124, and 146.)

Psalm 148:1-14

1 Praise the Lord. Praise the Lord from the heavens, praise him in the heights above.

2 Praise him, all his angels, praise him, all his heavenly hosts.

3 Praise him, sun and moon, praise him, all you shining stars.

4 Praise him, you highest heavens and you waters above the skies.

5 Let them praise the name of the Lord, for he commanded and they were created.

6 He set them in place forever and ever; he gave a decree that will never pass away.

7 Praise the Lord from the earth, you great sea creatures and all ocean depths,

8 lightning and hail, snow and clouds, stormy winds that do his bidding,

9 you mountains and all hills, fruit trees and all cedars,

10 wild animals and all cattle, small creatures and flying birds,

11 kings of the earth and all nations, you princes and all rulers on earth,

12 young men and maidens, old men and children.

13 Let them praise the name of the Lord, for his name alone is exalted; his splendor is above the earth and the heavens.

14 He has raised up for his people a horn, the praise of all his saints of Israel, the people close to his heart. Praise the Lord.

The Sunrise

Chances are the actual sunrise will be more meaningful than anything you could ever write. Don't try to come up with a message or sermon. Allow the beauty of creation to speak to your youth. As the sun begins to show, open the Bible to Genesis chapter one. Read the full creation story. You can play music as a background to the reading or wait until after the reading and then play the music.

Blessing/Closing

Option 1: Father God, we begin this new day with a new determination to be your children. *Amen.*

Option 2: The spirit of the Creator is here, and out there, and all around, and in you. *Amen.*

A Service for Morning

Style	Inspirational, affirming
Location	Preferably outdoors
Length	15 to 20 minutes
Materials	Bibles, boom box
Scripture	Isaiah 58:8-12, Isaiah 60:17-22, Psalm 126
Music Suggestions	Tracks 1 or 6 from the *Eucharist* CD or something "lively" of your own choosing. Geoff Moore & the Distance have some great, blood-pumping stuff on their *Greatest Hits* CD.
Comments/Ideas	You may need to adjust this service depending on whether or not you're on a mission trip or using it as a stand-alone service.

Introduction

Using the Morning Service as part of a mission week or summer camp—

One of the amazing things that happens during a mission week or summer camp is that the group begins to come together. So, by using the same order of worship each morning of your trip, the group will become comfortable with the responses and the "feel" of the service. Use the same Opening/Invocation each day. You can also use the same music or responsive reading to create a sense of familiarity away from home.

From that comfort comes an ease of participation. From the participation comes group building. If you're on a mission trip, you need to build a cohesive unit so they'll work well—and play well—together.

And getting them to worship well together is a big step in that direction.

Using the Morning Service as a stand-alone service—

The morning service is a great opportunity to refocus your group after a long night of giggling during a lock-in or if you're about to embark on an all-day journey.

You may have to use this as a "Charge!" service. If your students are grouchy and half-awake, use loud upbeat music. Ask them to shout the responses. Have students with infectious personalities read the Scriptures. Focus them on the task and the fact that this is a church event. Then charge them up for the journey.

Order of Worship

Opening Blessing

May God the Father and Jesus Christ his only Son, grant us renewal and energize our spirits for the coming day. Joy comes in the morning. *Amen.*

Prayer

Use one of these or choose a morning prayer from the Prayers section of the book.

Creator God, we can't begin to imagine all that you are or all that you've done for us. Each new morning is a new chance. A chance to put behind us all that we were and look ahead to all that we can be. You've brought us through another night. The darkness falls from our eyes and the wonders of your world become visible. Let us see your creation with the eyes of a child, God. Let it all be new to us again. Let us stand up and greet this day. Let us welcome it. Keep us from hiding from the sun because we are tired and weary. Your son rose in the morning and gave us all a new chance at life. Help us to take that chance. Help us to embrace this day with energy and passion. Let this be the start, God. *Amen.*

God, you made all things. In the glorious moments of creation, you gave us all that we need. The stars and the moon and the planets are all your handiwork. The animals that roam the earth and the trees that grow and the birds that soar in the sky are all from your hand. We are part of your creation, God. Help us to respect our world. Help us appreciate the natural gifts you've given us. The mountains push rise up before us. The oceans carry more life than we can imagine. But whether we're lodged in the deepest part of the city or alone in the desert, let us see the sunrise and realize how incredibly powerful you are. Help us stand and feel the warmth of the sun on our skin. Help us feel the incredible love you have for your children—just like we feel that warmth. Wrap your arms around us, God, and forgive us the stupid things we do to your world. *Amen.*

Responsive Reading

Use one of these responsive readings or choose one from the Responsive Readings section. Instruct your students to repeat the line after the leader reads the boldface line.

You can also pass the book around a circle so that each can speak one line aloud.

Option 1

Leader: Father, we stumble around in the dark.

Group: Shine your light, God.

Leader: We get lost and can't find the way.

Group: Shine your light, God.

Leader: We say things that hurt those we love.

Group: Shine your light, God.

Leader: We turn our backs on those who need us.

Group: Shine your light, God.

Leader: We turn our backs on you.

Group: Shine your light, God.

Leader: We get so lost.

Group: Shine your light, God.

Leader: We will follow the light.

Group: Shine your light, God.

Leader: A little at a time make the path clear for us.

Group: Shine your light, God.

Leader: Bring us out of the forest.

Group: Shine your light, God.

Leader: Show us your creation.

Group: Shine your light, God.

Leader: Hold our hands and let us walk with you.

Group: Shine your light, God.

Leader: Your word is a light for our path.

Group: Shine Your Light God.

Leader: *Amen.*

Option 2

Leader: We have come out of the darkness.

Group: We will celebrate this day.

Leader: God has forgiven us yet again.

Group: We will celebrate this day.

Leader: God has created this day for us.

Group: We will celebrate this day.

Leader: God has given us another day.

Group: We will celebrate this day.

Leader: Rain or sunshine—it doesn't matter

Group: We will celebrate this day.

Leader: Winter snow or heat of summer—it doesn't matter.

Group: We will celebrate this day.

Leader: We can make all things right.

Group: We will celebrate this day.

Leader: We can use this day to start again.

Group: We will celebrate this day.

Leader: We can take the first step.

Group: We will celebrate this day.

Leader: We can become new.

Group: We will celebrate this day.

Leader: We won't let it go to waste.

Group: We will celebrate this day.

Leader: We won't toss it aside.

Group: We will celebrate this day.

Leader: It's a gift from the creator of the universe.

Group: We will celebrate this day.

Leader: *Amen.*

Scripture Readings

Isaiah 58:8-12   God wants our "service" to others to become a route to personal growth.

Isaiah 60:17-22   A "coming attractions" verse about the Kingdom of God.

Psalm 126 (*interpreted*) A coming-out-of- the-dark psalm, written to celebrate deliverance from captivity.

God has brought us back. We were slaves, and now we are free.

We were caught in the dark, and now we are in the light again.

We will sing and dance and shout.

God loves us. God will work miracles for us because he loves us.

We ask God to bless us again.

We cried when we started because we had nothing.

Now the blessings of God are too many to count.

We cried when we started because we had nothing.

Now it's all good. It's all good.

Circle

Have your group form a circle. If your group is too large to form a circle, have your students spread out so they won't distract each other. Have the circle face outward, and tell them to fix their eyes on a point as far away in the distance as they can. Slowly begin to take in the wonders of creation that surround them. This should be done in silence.

Allow the silence to continue for as long as you like, or you can begin reading the creation story. Use your favorite Bible interpretation of Genesis 1:1 - 2:2.

{ 47 }

Music

Use tracks 1 or 6 from the Eucharist *CD or choose an appropriate piece to play on boom box or lead the group in singing.*

Closing Prayer

Father God, we are your creations. We stand here this morning in complete awe of all that you've done. You made the sky, you made the water, you made the rain and the sun. All life comes from you and the gifts that you give us. Let us begin our day with a living laughter that renews our bodies and heart and minds. Joy comes in the morning. Let us be renewed with the rising sun. Make our spirits new. *Amen.*

A Service for Sunset

Style	Meditative
Location	On a hilltop or rooftop
Length	15 minutes
Materials	Bible, boom box
Scripture	Psalm 19, 84, 104:1-19; Isaiah 60:19-20; Jeremiah 31:35
Music Suggestions	I've used everything from Geoff Moore to Johnny Cash. I have especially enjoyed *Officium* by the Hilliard Ensemble (17th-century monk chants accompanied by jazz saxophone). There's also a nice sunset piece by Tom Waits called "San Diego Serenade," but you might want to preview that one first.
Comments/Ideas	Just let it happen.

Introduction

There's an old saying that goes, "If your work speaks for itself, don't interrupt." That applies to this informal service. There isn't anything you can say that will make a sunset better. A sunset is some of God's best artistry—just let it speak for itself. You can talk before and after, but let God be God.

Timing is key here. Feel free to lead this service sitting on a hill with your group. The entire worship experience can be done in 15 minutes or less. Allow the sunset to act as the "message" or "sermon" of the service. Use the prayers and readings, and then allow the group to watch the sunset before reading the closing prayer.

Order of Worship

Opening

God, the sun is going down, and we have reached the end of another day. Watch over us through this night, Lord. Give us rest and peace. Reassure us of your love. You put the sun in the sky to rise and set. You gave us the day and the night. Help us to remember that. Help us to remember that you are the almighty God who set the moon in orbit. As we close this day, bring to our minds all those ways we've served you well. And forgive us for ways we've hurt each other today. As we watch the sky change color, give us peace of mind. *Amen.*

Scriptures

Assign these prior to the service or read them yourself.

Psalm 19:1-6, Psalm 84, Isaiah 60:19-20, Jeremiah 31:35, Psalm 104:1-19

Responsive Reading

Instruct your group to repeat the phrase, "The sun rises, and the sun sets" following the leader's statements.

Leader: The God of creation made the first day.

Group: The sun rises, and the sun sets.

Leader: Noah sat on the deck of his ark and watched a miracle.

Group: The sun rises, and the sun sets.

Leader: Joseph counted the days in his prison cell.

Group: The sun rises, and the sun sets.

Leader: David was inspired by beauty of the sky.

Group: The sun rises, and the sun sets.

Leader: The man born blind saw its beauty and praised God.

Group: The sun rises, and the sun sets.

Leader: Mary prayed at sunset until morning when she could go to Jesus' tomb.

Group: The sun rises, and the sun sets.

Leader: We watch the days pass one by one.

Group: The sun rises, and the sun sets.

Leader: We enter into the night.

Group: The sun rises, and the sun sets.

Leader: God will keep us safe.

Group: The sun rises, and the sun sets.

Leader: God will give us rest.

Group: The sun rises, and the sun sets.

Leader: God will give us peace of mind. *Amen.*

The Sunset

You can use an appropriate piece of music here if you have one. It's preferable to use something instrumental. Watching the sunset can trigger all sorts of daydreams and visions in teenagers. If you play music with vocals, it may distract them from letting their minds imagine naturally.

Closing Prayer

Father God, we are grateful for the gift of another day. You gave us another chance to serve you. You have given us another chance to be your children. Give us rest now, Lord. Keep us safe through the night, and we will honor you in the morning. *Amen.*

(◎⁓◎—

A Service for the Small Hours

Style	Meditative
Location	Inside or outside
Length	20 to 30 minutes
Materials	Bible, boom box, candles
Scripture	Genesis 1:16-18, 1 Kings 19: 9-13
Music Suggestions	For some reason this service works well with "high church" music. Also try *Officium* by the Hilliard Ensemble (17th-century monk chants accompanied by a jazz saxophone). There's also a CD entitled *The Prayer Cycle* that can work. The a capella vocals by Chanticleer is a great fit as well.
Comments/Ideas	Keep it small and dark.

Introduction

This service is written for use at night. It works best with groups of fewer than 20, but it can be used for larger groups as well. You can schedule this service into a lock-in or retreat as a Service for the Small Hours. You can schedule it or allow for a spontaneous service.

Sleep is rarely found at most overnight events. Very often you'll find yourself in one of those deep conversations about the meaning of life, the universe—you get the idea. This service requires no materials other than a candle, Bible, and boom box.

Track 8 on the *Eucharist* CD (in the back of this book) is a quiet, contemplative song. There are no lyrics. You can use this as an opener. Allow the group to sit in silence for a full minute before starting. When the music begins, light a single candle in the center of the circle.

Never Underestimate the Power of Candles!

Candles are wonderful worship tools. A single candle can shrink the size of a room. Candles create intimate settings in any location. With a single candle in a

dark room, there is no difference between your office and the sanctuary.

If you feel comfortable giving each of your youth candles, you can close the service by asking students to blow out their candles and stand in the darkness for a moment. Explain to them that they'll each be given an opportunity to pray for someone else in the group. After they've prayed, they are to walk across the circle and light that person's candle. The person receiving the flame then prays for someone else and walks across to light that person's candle. Continue this until every candle is lit. (Note: If there's someone in the group who might feel badly if his or her candle is the last lit, use your prayer to light that student's candle or invite that student to be first.)

The Sounds of Silence

Don't be afraid of silence. Nighttime services are made for quiet contemplation. Allow for times of complete silence between the pieces of the service. This will give your students time to "look inward" and focus on the candle.

Order of Worship

Opening Prayer

Option 1: God, we stand here in the quiet of the night. Grant us a peaceful conclusion to the day, and watch over us in the night as we sleep and dream. Be in our thoughts and souls as we turn over our hearts to you. *Amen.*

Option 2: God, the light of a single candle can illuminate the faces of all those in this circle. As this night begins, help us to remember that you created the darkness and the light for your own purposes. Whether it's day or night, we can't hide from your face. You know us too well. We are your children. Stay with us through the night, God. Bring us rest. Bring us renewal. We know that joy comes in the morning. *Amen.*

Option 3: Father in heaven, one light may not seem like much. But here a single candle will light another, the flame will spread, and soon we will illuminate the whole world. Light the flame of our hearts, Lord. In this world of darkness, let us be lights to others as your son is a light to us. *Amen.*

Responsive Reading

Instruct those in attendance to reply to each statement with either, "Thanks be to God" or "We thank you, God," depending on your preference.

Leader: God of light and our salvation, we gather in your name on this night.
Group: Thanks be to God.
Leader: We see the night sky and marvel at your creation.
Group: Thanks be to God.
Leader: For the all the laughter and time together
Group: Thanks be to God.
Leader: For the Scriptures and the lessons we learn.
Group: Thanks be to God.
Leader: For silly games and good friends
Group: Thanks be to God.
Leader: For music and candles
Group: Thanks be to God.
Leader: For warm hands to hold
Group: Thanks be to God.
Leader: For shoulders to lean on
Group: Thanks be to God.
Leader: For those who give their time and talents to this youth group
Group: Thanks be to God.
Leader: For all the things we take for granted during the week
Group: Thanks be to God.
Leader: For light and faith and hope
Group: Thanks be to God.
Leader: For your son, Jesus Christ. *Amen.*
Group: Thanks be to God.

Scripture Reading

Genesis 1:16-18

God made two great lights—the greater light to govern the day, and the lesser light to govern the night. He also made the stars. God set them in the expanse of the sky to give light on the earth, to govern the day and the night, and to separate light from darkness. And God saw that it was good.

1 Kings 19:9-13

There he went into a cave and spent the night. And the word of the Lord came to him: "What are you doing here, Elijah?"

He replied, "I have been very zealous for the Lord God Almighty. The Israelites have rejected your covenant, broken down your altars, and put your prophets to death with the sword. I am the only one left, and now they are trying to kill me, too."

The Lord said, "Go out and stand on the mountain in the presence of the Lord, for the Lord is about to pass by."

Then a great and powerful wind tore the mountains apart and shattered the rocks before the Lord, but the Lord was not in the wind. After the wind there was an earthquake, but the Lord was not in the earthquake. After the earthquake came a fire, but the Lord was not in the fire. And after the fire came a gentle whisper. When Elijah heard it, he pulled his cloak over his face and went out and stood at the mouth of the cave.

Then a voice said to him, "What are you doing here, Elijah?"

Music

Play an appropriate piece of music or have your group sing a quiet song.

Psalm 46

interpreted

Read this psalm "round robin" style. In other words, each member of your group gets to read one line until the psalm is completed. Pass the book around the circle or make copies prior to the service.

God is our fortress.

God is our protector.

Let the earth tremble

Let the mountains fall into the ocean.

Let the ocean's waves shake the earth.

Let the rivers roar into the city.

God is already there.

A mere flood will not shake the city.

Leaders of nations may shout

But the voice of God can make the earth itself melt.

God ends wars.

God breaks arrows, melts the guns, and silences the bombs.

God calls out to the nations, "Peace. Be still."

God is our fortress and protector.

Amen.

Message

optional

Closing Prayer

Option 1: If your group is small enough and you trust them with candles, pass unlit candles to them, keeping a single candle lit in the center of the circle. Explain that each person will take a turn praying silently for another member of the group and then light that person's candle. The person who has just received the flame then prays for someone else and lights that person's candle. Continue until all the candles are lit.

Option 2: If your group is too large or can't sit in a circle, have them focus on the light of a single candle in front of them. As they focus on the flame, ask them to think of one way they've wronged someone in the past. Allow them a moment to remember. Then blow out the candle and say, "Jesus forgives our sins."

Benediction/Blessing

Option 1: God, be with us as we travel through this night. Send your angels to watch over us and protect us. Grant us peace and rest so that we may serve you tomorrow. Your joy comes in the morning. *Amen.*

Option 2: God, be in our hearts this night. Keep the darkness from our souls and allow us to take the light with us as we dream. Speak to us, Lord. Your servants are listening. *Amen.*

Option 3 (*outdoors*): God as we stare at the night sky, we begin to understand how incredibly awesome you are. It was your hand that created the stars and the moon. It was at your word that the creatures of the night became a reality. Yet we're the ones you call "children." Help us somehow to be worthy of your love. Grant us rest and renewal and wake us with the sun. *Amen.*

A Service in the Rain

Style	Quietly inspirational
Location	Duh!
Length	20 minutes
Materials	Waterproof bulletins, boom box
Scripture	Deuteronomy 32:2; Jeremiah 10:13, 14:22; Psalm 135; Matthew 8:23-26, 14:22-31
Music Suggestions	Consider using "Flood" by Jars Of Clay. Other nice fits include "Have a Little Faith in Me" by Jewel or "To Make You Feel My Love," sung by Billy Joel (it can sound like the words of God). There's always "Let It Rain" by Eric Clapton if you have some classic rockers in your group. Or you can use a song of your own choosing.
Comments/Ideas	It might be a good idea to stay near a shelter in case things get really muddy or torrential.

Introduction

This is a great service that takes both pre-planning and spur-of-the-moment thinking. Create waterproof worship cards with the Order of Worship on one side and the Scripture readings on the reverse side. Use the given text or create your own service (and one for every student), then laminate them. Keep these cards on file, and if the weather report says you're in for a big one...hold the service in the pouring rain! A good suggestion for the music may be "Flood" by Jars of Clay.

The Message

When giving the message, talk about the fact that Jesus didn't sit in the boat next to Peter and say, "Go!" He stood in the stormy water and said, "Come." Emphasize that there comes a time when we all have to make the decision to step out of the boat. We may sink. Peter did. Don't feel bad if you have doubts. Jesus knows about them. He knew about Peter's doubts. (There's a reason they called Peter "The Rock"...he sank like a stone!) So if Peter—the very foundation on which the church was built—had doubts, why should we feel bad about our doubts? Don't feel bad if you have questions about your faith. Jesus will be there to lift us up and hold us. He will carry us back to the boat.

Order of Service

Opening Prayer

Scripture

Psalm 135

Responsive Reading

Instruct your group to reply, "We feel your love like the rain," after each leader statement.

Leader: Wash us clean God

Group: We feel your love like the rain

Leader: Life can be filled with storms

Group: We feel your love like the rain

Leader: Cleanse us of all the walls that we put up between each other, God
Group: We feel your love like the rain
Leader: Break through our barriers; drench us in your love
Group: We feel your love like the rain
Leader: Guide us through the storm
Group: We feel your love like the rain
Leader: Light the way
Group: We feel your love like the rain
Leader: Rain down so we don't drown in them
Group: We feel your love like the rain
Leader: Hear our cry in the storm
Group: We feel your love like the rain
Leader: Heal us
Group: We feel your love like the rain
Leader: *Amen.*

Music

Scripture

Matthew 14: 22-31; 8:23-26

Message

Closing Prayer

God, if the wind could blow away our problems, we would stand in a hurricane. If washing away the stress and chaos of our lives were merely a matter of standing in the rain, we would stand in the downpour and get drenched. If the wind could blow the sadness from our faces, we would face a hurricane. If it were that easy, God, we would never come out of the rain. Pour down your love and mercy on us, God. Renew us like the spring. Rain peace and justice on this crazy world. Drench us in your love. *Amen.*

Reverse Side

Deuteronomy 32:2
Let my teaching fall like rain and my words descend like dew,
like showers on new grass,
like abundant rain on tender plants.

Jeremiah 10:13
When he thunders, the waters in the heavens roar;
he makes clouds rise from the ends of the earth.
He sends lightning with the rain and brings out the wind from his storehouses.

Jeremiah 14:22
Do any of the worthless idols of the nations bring rain?
Do the skies themselves send down showers?
No, it is you, O Lord our God.
Therefore our hope is in you,
for you are the one who does all this.

A Memorial Service for a Youth Group Member

Style	Memorial
Location	Outdoors, roof of the church
Length	20 to 30 minutes
Materials	Bibles, helium balloons, boom box
Scripture	Isaiah 25:6-9, 61:1-3; Lamentations 3:22-33; Job 19:21-27; Psalms 23, 27, 42, 46, 90, 106, 116, 212, 130, 139; John 14:1-6; Romans 8:14-39; 1 Corinthians 15:20-58; 2 Corinthians 4:16-5:9; 1 John 3:1-2
Music Suggestions	A song the deceased really liked. (Also "Listen to Our Hearts" by Geoff Moore & The Distance and "The 23rd Psalm" by Bobby McFerrin.)
Comments/Ideas	Don't restrict emotions.

Introduction

It's my hope and prayer that you'll never have to lead this service. But the Scriptures and liturgies can be of great comfort in a time when we're asking the hard "why?" questions.

Create this service for your youth group only, but be sure to invite the family of the deceased member. You may want to invite your senior pastor to take part in the service, but do as much as you can to make it a service for the youth group to grieve one of its own. If you don't have a lot of grief counseling experience, it's good to have someone on hand who does.

If you can, hold this service in a location that was the favorite of the deceased. It doesn't matter if you're in a McDonald's parking lot or by the ocean. It's important to establish the location as part of the service.

Part of this service includes releasing helium balloons. If balloons aren't available, use candles, though you may have to move the service indoors if the weather is bad.

Remember that your students are trying to act like adults at a time like this. They are trying to be grown up about the death of their friend. Meanwhile the grownups are trying to "be strong for the children" and may not let their emotions show. What results is a painful cycle. The teenagers are looking at the adults not crying and the adults are thinking, "Why aren't the kids grieving?" Hopefully this service can break down some of these walls.

If at all possible, use music the deceased enjoyed. Get copies of the discs from other youth group members and find a few appropriate pieces.

Above all else, allow the tears.

Before the Service

Pass out the helium balloons. If you're inside and using candles, light a candle in the front of the room or the center of the circle.

Order of Worship

Opening Prayer

Creator God, we remember _____ this day. _____ wasn't with us long enough. We thank you for the time we got spend with (him/her). (His/her) family, friends are grateful for the time we got to walk beside _____ on the path. Focus our minds and hearts on (his/her) life. Let us celebrate each moment that we had with _____. Ease our pain until we're together again in your house. *Amen.*

Reading

God, _____ is home. _____ has already walked into your loving arms and felt the embrace of your son.

To those of us left here, give us the faith to stay on the path.

Give us courage to face coming days without _____.

Give us the strength to pray in the face of things we don't understand.

Give us the strength to believe in the forgiveness and mercy you promised us all.

Give us the grace to entrust _____ to you.

Give us the ever-increasing knowledge of you and your son so that we may one day understand why you take those who have so much living left to do.

Invite _____ to your table.

Serve _____ (his/her) favorite foods.

Play music that _____ loves.

Give _____ eyes that can see we how much we miss (him/her).

Give us eyes to see (his/her) smile in the sunrise.

Give us the ears to hear (his/her) voice in the rain.

Give peace to (his/her) family and friends, God, and to (his/her) restless spirit, and to the world.

Amen.

Responsive Reading

Instruct your group to reply, "Lord, bring _____ home" (insert the name of the person who has passed away) after each leader statement.

Leader: God, we gather here because we loved _____.

Group: Lord, bring _____ home.

Leader: _____ was our friend and will be missed.

Group: Lord, bring _____ home.

Leader: It hurts to lose someone, God.

Group: Lord, bring _____ home.

Leader: We know _____ is with you, but there is an empty space down here.

Group: Lord, bring _____ home.

Leader: The time we have on this earth is short.

Group: Lord, bring _____ home.

Leader: The time span of our lives is merely a spoon of water in the ocean when we compare it to what you have in store for us.

Group: Lord, bring _____ home.

Leader: Hold _____.

Group: Lord, bring _____ home.

Leader: Help us to live our lives without _____ here.

Group: Lord, bring _____ home.

Leader: Help us go on.

Group: Lord, bring _____ home.

Leader: Help us have the faith that we will see _____ again.

Group: Lord, bring _____ home.

All: *Amen.*

Scripture—Old Testament

Read one or more of the following Scriptures.

Isaiah 25:6-9 (death is no more)

Isaiah 61:1-3 (the grieving will find comfort)

Lamentations 3:22-33 (God is good)

Job 19:21-27 (God is real)

Psalms

Other suitable psalms for memorial services include 23, 27, 46, 90, 106, 116, 130, and 139.

Psalm 42

interpreted

As the animals of the woods get thirsty for the cool streams, so do I get thirsty for God.

God, I need to know you are there.

I need to see your face.

I feel like I have no more tears left, God.

My heart feels like it's made of broken stone.

I hear the voices in the sanctuary singing joyful songs, and I am not happy.

Why can't I stop pacing, God?

You are good to me, God.

When I wake in the morning 'til I sleep at night.

You are good to me.

You give me music to dance to.

When my life is a hurricane, you are the rock I cling to.

I don't want to feel sad anymore, God.

But I will trust you.

Lift me from the hole.

You are my God.

Amen.

Psalm 121—A Prayer for Protection

Have two readers take turns with this interpreted psalm.

Reader 1: I am standing alone in an empty field. Three is nothing as far as I can see. Where is the help? Where will my help come from?

Reader 2: God is watching. God is standing over you like a playground monitor. God will not let you stumble. God will not let you fall. God will be your shade in the heat of the day. God will be your warm blanket at night. God will protect you from all dangers.

God will be with you always.

Reader 1: I am standing alone in an empty field. There is nothing as far as I can see. Where is the help? Where will my help come from?

Scripture—New Testament

Choose one or more of the New Testament readings.

John 14:1-6 (It's a big, big house.)

Romans 8:14-39 (God will show us what it's all about.)

1 Corinthians 15:20-58 (The body is nothing. God has something better.)

2 Corinthians 4:16-5:9 (What is unseen is what lasts.)

1 John 3:1-2 (We shall be like him.)

A Time for Remembering

At this time ask anyone who would like so share a memory or reading to do so.

Helium Balloons

Explain that the balloons are a symbol of our attachment to the one we lost. As long as we have memories, that person will never really be gone from us. After the closing prayer, explain that the students are welcome to stay as long as they'd like. When they're ready to leave, simply "let go" and leave silently.

If you're using candles, invite the group to come forward and take a small candle, light it from the main candle, and return to their seat for the closing prayer.

Closing Prayer

You can use this prayer or speak from your heart and allow God to give you the words.

Creator God, we don't understand. Perhaps we aren't meant to. We will stop asking the questions and celebrate the arrival of _____ into your house. We know the banquet table was already prepared with plenty of (_____ *favorite food*). We know that (_____ *favorite band*) is playing at an incredible volume. We know that _____ is in the stars, so happy and free, telling us not to be sad, and that (he/she) can't wait to be with us again. And we all will see him again someday. Stay with us, God. Make the ache go away a little bit more each day. Let us keep the memories. Let us keep the light. *Amen.*

A Service for a National Tragedy

Style	Memorial-like, prayerful, meditative
Location	Sanctuary or chapel
Length	Usually 30 to 40 minutes
Materials	None are needed
Scripture	Psalms 23, 46, 54, 72, 80, 121; Matthew 5:1-12; Isaiah 61:1-3
Music Suggestions	"Amazing Grace" is good. Or any song that emphasizes the awesomeness of God or faith and trust in God.
Comments/Ideas	Play it by ear.

Introduction

More than likely, you won't have much time to prepare for this service. In order to capture what you're after, you'll usually have less than 48 hours after the event to create this service and get the word out about it. After national tragedies, it's a good idea to open your church to the community at large.

This is a prayer service. During times when our country is being affected by something larger than ourselves, we often ask, "What can I do?" The answer is almost always "pray." This service focuses on the power of prayer. It helps to hold the service in a church or some place

that's already conducive to corporate prayer. But if there's a location that'll work better, use it. After the Columbine shootings, for instance, I held a service in a local high school parking lot.

Option: Psalm 23 and "Amazing Grace" are two highly recognizable worship tools. They are familiar even to those who don't attend church. As such, they provide a link between regular churchgoers and unchurched people. Using these two expressions of prayer and worship puts everyone on familiar ground at a time when nothing is familiar.

The Service

Welcome

Begin by stating the obvious. Tell those who've showed up the reason you've gathered. Of course they already know, but hearing it stated aloud creates a connection between those in attendance. Some people may be complete strangers. Stating why you're together can quickly bond everybody together.

Opening Prayer

Creator God, we come to you in confusion. Our minds argue with our hearts, and we are full of doubts and questions. More than anything else we need your blessed assurance. We ask that you be with the families of (those involved in the tragedy). We are your children, God, and we like things in neat, little packages. None of this makes sense to us, God. We invite your Holy Spirit to come and comfort us, as well as those in (location of the tragedy). Be with us, God. *Amen.*

Music

Scriptures

Matthew 5:1-12, Isaiah 61:1-3

A Reading from the Psalms

Chose from one or more of the psalms listed at the end of the service.

Responsive Reading

Simply instruct those present to repeat, "God, we need to know you are there," after the leader statements.

Leader: God, we've read the newspapers.

Group: God, we need to know you are there.

Leader: We've seen the video footage.

Group: God, we need to know you are there.

Leader: We talk about faith.

Group: God, we need to know you are there.

Leader: Our brains demand evidence.

Group: God, we need to know you are there.

Leader: Our hearts long to believe.

Group: God, we need to know you are there.

Leader: Forgive us our doubts, God.

Group: God, we need to know you are there.

Leader: The world is a cruel place.

Group: God, we need to know you are there.

Leader: The hungry and hurting reach out.

Group: God, we need to know you are there.

Leader: The questions and doubts rise up like a raging river.

Group: God, we need to know you are there.

Leader: We could drown in our own ignorance.

Group: God, we need to know you are there.

Leader: Come into this place.

Group: God, we need to know you are there.

Leader: We will open our hardened hearts.

Group: God, we need to know you are there.

Leader: We will open our minds and souls.

Group: God, we need to know you are there.

Leader: Show us.

Group: God, we need to know you are there.

Leader: Enlighten us.

All: God, we need to know you are there

A Reading

Give us faith to stay on the path.

Give us the courage to face the coming days.

Give us the strength to pray in the face of things we don't understand

Give us the strength to believe in the mercy and grace you've promised us all.

Give us the grace to entrust to you those we lost.

Invite them to your table.

Serve them their favorite foods.

Give them eyes to see how much we miss them.

Give us the eyes to see their smiles in the sunrise.

Give us the ears to hear their voices in the rain.

Give peace to their family and friends, and to the world.

Amen.

Music

The Prayer Circle

Ask the congregation or group to form a circle, preferably around the altar or around the sanctuary. If yours is a congregation with more than 100 members, you may want to make more than one circle. Have the group hold hands. Explain that they're in no way required to pray aloud. Explain that a silent prayer is heard as well as one spoken out loud. Each person will be asked to pray. When one person is done, she simply squeezes the hand of the person next to her, then it's his turn to pray...and so on. If you are the worship leader, then you should go last.

Let those in the circle know that this is why they're here. They are gathered to lift their prayers to God. There is no time limit or word limit. If you happen to have a tradition-ally long-winded person in your circle...just let them talk.

Psalm 23

Music

Closing Prayer

Creator God, the hardest part about being your children is that we don't get to see the big picture. You see everything. You know how it all turns out in the end. You see the completed puzzle while we sit here with one small piece in our hands and cry. Give us the faith to believe that you have it all under control. Give us the strength to get up and move on in the morning. Give us the love to support each other. We want to run into you arms and have you hold us like children. Tell us it's going to be okay. Hold us, God. It's lonely down here right now. *Amen.*

The Psalms

These psalms are often thought to be psalms of encouragement. Some of them here have been adapted for two readers.

Psalm 46

interpreted for two readers

Angry voice: My God is a castle on a mountain. I am safe. The entire planet can rumble under my feet. Oceans can boil Waves crash into my mountain I won't be afraid.

Calm voice: There is a river that flows in my mountain. It brings joy. It brings love. God is here. This mountain isn't going anywhere.

Angry voice: Nations rage against each other.

Calm voice: Their damage is nothing.

Angry voice: God need only whisper a word, and the planet will dissolve. People get angry. They throw things. Fire guns. Drop bombs.

Calm voice: God says, "Hush." Be still. I am here. And the world will be silent. *Amen.*

Psalm 80

a prayer for the nations

interpreted

God you watch over us from your house.
Your angels fly around you.
You play hackysack with the sun.
Down here, things have gone from bad to worse.
You gave us all we needed.
You put us in the right place at the right time.
Still our enemies laugh at us.
Help us again, God.
Pull us from this mess we've made.
We will praise your name.
Smile on us again.
Save us from ourselves.
Amen.

Psalm 72

a prayer for the leaders of our country

1 Endow the king with your justice, O God, the royal son with your righteousness.

2 He will judge your people in righteousness, your afflicted ones with justice.

3 The mountains will bring prosperity to the people, the hills the fruit of righteousness.

4 He will defend the afflicted among the people and save the children of the needy; he will crush the oppressor.

5 He will endure as long as the sun, as long as the moon, through all generations.

6 He will be like rain falling on a mown field, like showers watering the earth.

7 In his days the righteous will flourish; prosperity will abound 'til the moon is no more.

8 He will rule from sea to sea and from the river to the ends of the earth.

9 The desert tribes will bow before him, and his enemies will lick the dust.

10 The kings of Tarshish and of distant shores will bring tribute to him; the kings of Sheba and Seba will present him gifts.

11 All kings will bow down to him and all nations will serve him.

12 For he will deliver the needy who cry out, the afflicted who have no one to help.

13 He will take pity on the weak and the needy and save the needy from death.

14 He will rescue them from oppression and violence, for precious is their blood in his sight.

15 Long may he live! May gold from Sheba be given him. May people ever pray for him and bless him all day long.

16 Let grain abound throughout the land; on the tops of the hills may it sway. Let its fruit flourish like Lebanon; let it thrive like the grass of the field.

17 May his name endure forever; may it continue as long as the sun. All nations will be blessed through him, and they will call him blessed.

18 Praise be to the Lord God, the God of Israel, who alone does marvelous deeds.

19 Praise be to his glorious name forever; may the whole earth be filled with his glory. Amen and *Amen.*

Psalm 72

interpreted

Guide our leaders' decisions, God.

They are human.

Let them be honest and kind.

Be their example.

Show them the truth.

Let them care for those who cannot care for themselves.

Let them create a world of peace.

Let them be as helpful as rain on dry grass.

Let there be peace until the moon goes out.

Guide our leaders' decisions, God.

Amen.

Psalm 54:1-7

1 Save me, O God, by your name; vindicate me by your might.

2 Hear my prayer, O God; listen to the words of my mouth.

3 Strangers are attacking me; ruthless men seek my life—men without regard for God. Selah

4 Surely God is my help; the Lord is the one who sustains me.

5 Let evil recoil on those who slander me; in your faithfulness destroy them.

6 I will sacrifice a freewill offering to you; I will praise your name, O Lord, for it is good.

7 For he has delivered me from all my troubles, and my eyes have looked in triumph on my foes.

Psalm 121

interpreted for two readers

Reader 1: I am standing alone in an empty field. There is nothing as far as I can see. Where is the help? Where will my help come from?

Reader 2: God is watching. God is standing over you like a playground monitor. God will not let you stumble. God will not let you fall. God will be your shade in the heat of the day. God will be your warm blanket at night. God will protect you from all dangers. God will be with you always.

Prayers

In this section, you'll find dozens of prayers to use for services and devotions. They are listed in alphabetical order. Some of the prayers are written specifically for one service. Others can be used in a variety of services and situations.

Acceptance

LORD, we stand in the middle of your kingdom and wonder where it is. We forget that everyone is part of the kingdom, even those we don't like. Your son sat and ate with tax collectors and prostitutes. So we wonder—if we saw him today, would we welcome him into our homes knowing the company he keeps? Kill our egos, God. Sometimes we act like we own the kingdom. We make up rules and say they're yours. We pronounce judgments and say they're from your lips. Wake us up, Father. Help us. Open our eyes so we may see the world as your son saw it. Open our minds to see the possibilities we shut out. Open our hearts so that we may love as Jesus loved, without judgment or condition. Open our lives so that we may accept the rest of the world as Jesus accepts us. *Amen.*

Advent/Christmas

FATHER IN HEAVEN, we so often forget why we're doing this. We forget that hope is the reason you sent your son to us. We see the nightly news. We read the headlines. And we fear how the world will treat us when we engage it. Then we remember your son. We remember that Jesus came into this world to bring hope to people like us—people who feel the world's hopelessness. Father, sometimes we feel so far from you that our loneliness absolutely consumes us. Then we remember the Christ child. We remember that you brought us hope. Help us to hold high the light of Christ's hope, to hold it up as a beacon to bring the world out of darkness. *Amen.*

LORD, remind us to laugh. Remind us of when pure joy was a natural state. Let us remember when we were children. When we felt joy over our ice cream, Charlie Brown cartoons, and snow. Let us be joyful without looking over our shoulders. Let us show others that our joy comes from you and that the decorations, presents, and carols are merely expressions of you living inside us. Help us show joy to everyone. Help us realize that our joy may lead others to joyful relationships with you. *Amen.*

LORD, grant us peace when we worry about trying to shop and not having enough money to buy the things we want to for our friends and family. Grant us the peace to remember that the spirit of Christmas dwells in our homes and hearts and not in the mall. Grant us the peace to understand that the true gift of Christmas doesn't come from a store but comes from your son, the Prince of Peace, the reason we celebrate. *Amen.*

DEAR GOD, the presents are almost all wrapped. The shopping is almost done. All we have left is the waiting. So help us remember that the waiting is as much a blessing as the holiday. Help us use these days of preparation to ready ourselves for the arrival of your son. Help us make those around us aware that the waiting is a celebration. That the anticipation of Christmas will make it even more joyous. So let us burst with joy as the shepherds did. Let us sing like the angels did. Let us open our eyes and ears to the sights and the sounds of the season and open our hearts to the glory and wonder of the baby Jesus. *Amen.*

FATHER GOD, a candle is but one small light. One small light in a dark room will only light so much of it. In the same way, one little baby in born in stable went unnoticed by the rest of the city—but those who were called to that stable took the light they witnessed back into the world with them. So let us take a small piece of this light in our hearts. Let us show it to others so we can make it grow. Let our lights grow so bright that they can be seen from outer space. Jesus began as one small light in a dark stable in a dark town. He brought light to a dark world. He brought light to our lives. God, let us take that light now. *Amen.*

All Hallows Eve

GOD, forgive our selfishness. Forgive us for wanting our lost friends to be with us and not with you. This world gets cold sometimes, God. And then we feel alone. But when someone dies, it leaves an awful hole in our lives. We know the time we spend on earth isn't even a blink of an eye compared to the eternity we'll spend with you. This night is about you, God. It's not about vampires and candy bars. We celebrate the memory of those who've left this world to be with you. We miss them, but we know they are in your loving arms and that someday we'll all be together at your table. *Amen.*

WE MISS OUR FRIENDS, GOD. We miss our family members. We miss the warmth of their hugs. We know they're with you. We know they have long ago forgiven us all the nasty things we said to them. They watch us, and they laugh at our doubts and fears because now they are with you. They are no longer sick or in pain. They are brand new. We will continue to miss them. We will morn our losses, but we will do so knowing our loved ones are so incredibly alive that we can't comprehend it. We'll be sad, but we also know we will see them again. We will hold their hands and hug them and walk in the stars. Calm our sad hearts and minds, God. *Amen.*

Close of the Day

ANOTHER DAY IS DONE, FATHER. We hope we helped create a world you're proud of. As your children we want you to be happy with us. You gave us the planet as a gift, and we must care for it. We must cherish the people in our lives. Allow us to meditate on these things as we head into the night, God. Today is nearly over, and we can do nothing to change any of it. Give us rest, God. Give us peace. When the sun comes up in the morning, we will honor you. We will support and love each other, and we will show the world what it means to be a child of God. *Amen.*

THE SUN HAS SET, GOD. And the darkness that descends at nighttime makes the world smaller. We become less aware of things far away from us, and we become more aware of things close to us. We see our friends' faces. We see the light in the eyes of our loved ones. We feel the presence of the Holy Spirit moving through this circle. Help us stop worrying for now. Help us put it aside in the dark and leave it alone. The music surrounds us like your loving arms. Hold us close. Let us feel your warm reassuring hand on our shoulders and tell us it's going to be okay. Thank you for this day, God. Thank you for the new day we will open our eyes to in the morning. *Amen.*

Courage

GOD, it doesn't take bravery to follow the crowd. When the rest of the group says we're cowards because we don't participate in something we know is wrong, we only become cowards when we believe them. We are brave by design, God. You made us with the courage already inside. Obstacles were put on this earth so we could have something to overcome, so we could be stronger. It takes maturity to stand in the face of temptation and say, "no." We strive for that God. We don't want to be seen as children, so help us put away the childish decisions. Help us to be brave. *Amen.*

IT TAKES COURAGE TO STARE INTO THE DARKNESS, GOD. It seems like we can stand up to anything except the unknown. We know the monsters under the bed aren't real. What we fear is the sound of our parent's arguing. What we fear are the choices we have to make that will decide our future. And we can face the future like we're tiptoeing into the shallow end of the pool, or we can do a cannonball off the diving board. Let us be brave, God. Let us face the unknown. Help us stare down the darkness with a sense of wonder instead of a sense of apprehension. *Amen.*

Determination

GOD, it's easier than ever to get sidetracked. We are all citizens of the kingdom. We each have to make the decision as to how we will travel. The path that shines and gives us a new car may not be the easiest one. The path to you is hard, the road is uneven, and we have to walk. From where we're standing, we can't see the end of either choice. Give us faith, God. Give us strength and patience. Give us the willpower to walk away from the easy ride and start out on foot. The way of the world will eventually put us into the ditch or off the edge of a curving mountain road. The way of the kingdom is hard going but we will never have to walk it alone. Jesus is beside us. He offers encouragement. He offers his hand to hold. He offers rest in the shade when we can't go on any longer. God please give us just one, small glimpse of the kingdom so that we can renew our journey and stay on the path. *Amen.*

Easter

FATHER GOD, sometimes it feels like we've spent our whole lives waiting. Like the disciples, we sit together because we know something is going to happen. We stay locked in our rooms afraid to go out, afraid to move forward, afraid to look back. Send the Holy Spirit into our hearts like you sent the spirit into the upper room of the disciples. Come into our hearts like a storm inside a closed room. Change everything. Pick us up and spin us around and make everything new. Give us that one moment when all things are possible, and we feel like we can do anything in your name. Give us chance and let us show you that we can change your world. We can be the creations who honor their Creator. Turn our lives upside down, God. Make us new. *Amen.*

Enemies

GOD, there are people who don't like us. There are people down here who just seem to want to see our pain for the pure joy of it. It's so hard to pray for them, God. Then again, Jesus just said to do it. He didn't say it would be easy. We all feel like our lives are missing something, God. If there's one thing we all have in common, it's that we don't always feel complete. Those who like to see us hurt must have a huge hole inside them. They must ache in ways we couldn't possibly begin to understand. Fill their lives, God. Give them what they need. They have pain. They have insecurities. Maybe if you give them what they need they will leave us alone. And maybe they'll come to know you. Whatever they're not getting, God, please give it to them. Then come talk with us and explain how this all works. *Amen.*

CREATOR GOD, show us the mercy you promised, but let it be equal to the mercy we show to our worst detractors. There are people out there willing to line up and throw things at us, God. How can we love them? How can we show mercy to the ones who tried to make our lives miserable? Your son did it. Jesus hung from the cross and forgave those who put him there. People speak out against you, say you don't exist, and distort your Word for their own advancement, and you still call them your children. People tell lies about us, and it's hard not to fight back. We will pray for our enemies, God. We pray you give them whatever they need so they'll stop being so angry. We pray you heal them from their problems. Show them that you love them. Make your presence known to them as you have made it known to us time and time again. *Amen.*

Family

GOD, when families get along, it's like a sweet smell from the kitchen. When families work together, it's like summer day with the windows down and a good song on the radio. But families are made of people, God. We all have fears and doubts. We all have joys and expectations. Help us to bring all those into focus. Help us see the ways we can laugh together instead of the ways we clash like fingernails on chalkboards. Give us the space when we need it, even if it's in the middle of a crowded room. Help us to hold our tongues and not say things to hurt each other. We are family. We care for each other. Help us to get along with those we are closest to. *Amen.*

Faith

GOD, give us faith. When we're failing every class, give us faith. When we slip and fall in front of that one person we hope will like us, give us faith. When the rest of the world says, "Don't bother, it's too late, you're wasting your time," give us faith. Let us come to you confident that you'll answer us. Don't let it even be a question in our minds. You will help us. You will be there for us. You will listen to our problems and know exactly what we need. Help us hand life's difficulties over to you, Lord. Help us stop trying to solve our problems once we give them to you. Help us let go of them. Give us the faith to understand that you'll solve our problems in your time, not ours. Give us patience and understanding—and help us to be as patient and understanding with others as you have been with us. *Amen.*

FATHER GOD, we live our lives each day feeling like a block tower built by little children. The world is full of hard winds and shaky floors. We sense it could all crash down at any moment. But there is a foundation. Christ is the cornerstone. Christ will bear our burdens. In him we find the strength to stand up to the forces that try to destroy us, bring us down, and watch us crumble. Christ is our support. We need faith to give him our lives, and he will not let us fall. We are the church. We will build upon the cornerstone, and we will become the cathedral for the world. We will be a shelter for the homeless. We will be a school to teach our children. We will be a place of comfort for the aged. Christ is the cornerstone. We are the church. *Amen.*

Final Exams

WHY DO THEY DO THIS TO US, GOD? Why do they put so much importance on the grades we receive at the time of the year when we least want to study for them? Why do they judge us this way? Sometimes it feels like we're stuck inside a balloon. We can't even punch our way out. Give us eyes that stay focused when we're tired. Give us attention spans longer that the most boring lecture. Gives brains that hold information, if only long enough to spit it back onto a bubble graph. There is more beyond this. There are more tests. There are more challenges. There are more classes. There are more lessons. Give us patience. We are almost done. Exams are not trivial things, as some seem to think. Above all else give us the assurance that we're not alone. You never said life would be easy. But you did say we would never be alone. Let us feel your loving presence God. We are going to need it. *Amen.*

First Day of School

IT ALL STARTS AGAIN, GOD. We remember when we were kids, and we approached the first day of school with joy. Now we're not so sure. We look forward to seeing our friends. The summer can get boring. We also stand here a bit uneasy. This year will be harder than the last. This year we are different people than we were last year. Let this year be amazing, God. We don't ask that it be easy. We ask that it be amazing. If we always walked the easy path, we would miss the wondrous beauty that goes with climbing over the mountain. Don't let us be alone. Even when we screw up royally, don't let us be alone. It's almost here. Walk with us now the way we used to walk to the first day of school with our parents...hand in hand. Be with us, God. *Amen.*

Forgiveness

GOD, you did not send your son so that we'd do things the same old ways. Jesus didn't come into our lives so we'd be stuck in rut. Help us see things with the eyes of a child. Help us to stop looking over our shoulders and look ahead for what's to come. Each morning is a new day and a new chance for us to see all the opportunities that you give us. We spend a lot of time worrying about how we mess up. We're afraid that you won't love us anymore, and we try to hide from you. But like a loving father you wrap your arms around us. You forgive us and send us on our way with yet another chance. Stay with us, God. The path is long, and we need you to light the way so we don't stray from your direction. *Amen.*

GOD, the message is for us. Forgive us when we forget that. We think of ourselves as the ones who've been "saved," but we're no better. We forget we're the ones who must take the message to the world. We forget that we are your servants. When the banquet is prepared in your home, we expect to sit at the table next to you—but we will feel lucky to be the waiters. To eat the scraps and crumbs from the floor next to the dogs. Forgive us our selfishness God. Show us your kingdom here on earth. Show us the table, and we will serve your people now. Lighten our hearts and lessen our egos and let us show the world that we are worthy of being called the servants of the living God. *Amen.*

Gifts

GOD, we belong to you. You have given us wonderful gifts. The sunshine, the rain, the color of the sky—these are all gifts from you. You have given gifts to each of us individually. You have called us to be prophets, preachers, singers, artists, and leaders. We will answer that call. We will take the gifts you have given us, and we will use them for your good. We will work together the way the sun and the rain work together to grow the trees. We will hold each other up when we get tired. We will protect each other from the storm. We will guide each other when we're lost. We will follow Christ. He will lead us. He will keep us on the right path. When Christ appears, we will be graceful. We will be new. We will be like him. We are the body of Christ. *Amen.*

God Is in Charge

GOD, help us remember that your name always should be exalted—but that we won't get your attention by merely praying louder. We are your servants, God. Show us the direction in which you want us to go, and we will go. We are all your children. We must pray for everyone, even for those who don't look like us or think like us or believe as we do. Help us not feel so full of ourselves that we forget who's in charge. Let us understand that being your children also means being your servants, that loving you means also loving those who hurt us, and that being a child of God also means being changed on the inside. *Amen.*

GOD, you always have been. You always will be. You are in charge, not us. From heaven you rule the angels and the ants. You are the only God. Let there be no mistake. We have every reason to be shaking in our boots. Yet we know you love us beyond measure, but you won't always give us what we want. You will always give us what we need. You know our insecurities and our offenses. You've called your servants to walk through the fire before. They obeyed, and you protected them from the flames. We will praise you, God. You are the only God. *Amen.*

God's Law

GOD, we complain too much about the rules. You gave us the sunshine, and we celebrate it. You gave us the rain and we rejoice in that, too. Even the sky reveals all the gifts you give us. You hand us a world with everything we need to be happy, then you give us your laws and we complain like children. Everything that comes from you is good. Because with your laws, you give us wisdom. With wisdom you give us the ability to choose our own paths. It's hard to see our own failures, God. Keep us safe. Don't let the world tell us what's good, pure, and true. We know the things that come from you are what matter. We will rejoice in your laws, like we rejoice in the rain that ends a drought. We will rejoice in your laws the way we rejoice in the sunrise after a long, dark night. Make our actions acceptable to you, God. Help us to show the world the truth about your love. *Amen.*

Goodness

GOD, a careless word from our mouths can ruin someone's day, throw mud on a reputation, and turn harmony into chaos. Help us to think before we speak, God. Make us the kind of people who understand the power of words. Give us hearts of love so that we may reflect to the world what is inside us. We can't stick a cup into a pool of muck and come up with clear water. Make us clean on the inside, God, so that when we tell the world about your love, they don't run away. Make us worthy. Sit beside us. Show us the way. Create clean hearts in us, God, and your children will honor you. *Amen.*

{ 74 }

Good Times

GOD, nobody thinks about you when times are good. But when our lives are in the pit, we pray to you. We ask for your help. We have all the faith in the world that the bad stuff happens for a reason. Now, Father, our lives seem to be on track. Our grades are tolerable. Our future looks bright. We have some money in our pockets. Life is good. This is a gift from you, God. Thank you for the gift of youth. Thank you for this time when we're not bogged down by the pressures that pull at the corners of our parents' mouths. Thank you for life. Thank you for the joy and energy we experience so naturally. *Amen.*

Government

GOD, our leaders are human. We give them the authority to make decisions for the world. But they are human beings—just like us. Make them wise, God. Make them honest and kind. Give them courage. They make choices that none of us would ever want to make. Guide them. Be their example. Show them that all things work together for good for those who love you. We want to show the world that love is stronger than hate. That belief in you is stronger than indifference toward you. That light is stronger than darkness. Fill our leaders with wisdom, God. Place a reassuring hand on their shoulders when they make decisions. Let them see with clear eyes and them listen with open minds and hearts. Give them strength. Give us all strength. *Amen.*

Grace

GOD, we don't deserve the blessings you give us. We are your children, and you give us gifts of love and peace. You give us green grass and blue sky and all the seasons. You give us this wonderful earth and surround it with stars. There are miracles all around us, God. Many people write them off as chance and coincidence, but we know they are your handiwork. Too often we live as closed people, God. Help us open up to the miraculous so that miracles will happen. Help us believe so you can show us more of yourself. Give us the faith to take your word as truth, even without proof, so you can show us all we need to see to believe. *Amen.*

GOD, we give to the poor. We donate our old clothes. We come to church and pray. And we think we're earning points to get into heaven. We forget that we are already yours. We forget that your son has already settled the bill. We are already in. Grace is a gift from you, and we had no part in it. If we did we'd probably mess it up along with everything else in our lives. The only way we can say thank you is by how we live our lives. We stand in the spotlight of a thousand suns, so why do we choose to remain in the dark? It's only by our faith in Jesus that we can come to really know how much you've done for us. It's only by your mercy that we can teach the world. It's only by your mercy that your creations can do the work you created them to do. *Amen.*

Gratitude

GOD, thank you for the gift of life. Thank you for the ordinary stuff—walking around, sleeping, eating, drinking—you've given us. We know these gifts are from you. And to show our appreciation, we want to give them back to you. We will take all the seemingly small, meaningless pieces and place them before you. Nothing is meaningless to you, God. Nothing is trivial. We are new creations. You will take our baggage and selfish attitudes and throw them away. Your love pours down on the earth like a waterfall. We will stand at the bottom and become clean. We will show our gratitude by using our gifts to show others where they came from. We will share our talents and gifts with the rest of the world. Your children will make you proud, God. We will make you smile.

Grief

GOD, there's an ache that no medicine can heal. We feel the pain of loss, and we know there's nothing we can do about it. It feels like it will last forever. We know all the "right" things to say, God. We have the faith that those who leave this world will be with you and feel the love and the joy you promised. But that doesn't make it easier right now, God. Time is a healer. After a time, we will remember their face and smile instead of weep. After a time we will stop listening for their voice on the phone or from another room. After a time we will accept that we can't see them again in this lifetime. But there is another lifetime to come. It's an existence beyond what we can comprehend. We know our loss is heaven's gain. We believe that Jesus was there to welcome them into his strong carpenter's arms. We will ache, God. We bury a piece of ourselves with them. We won't get that piece back again—but someday we won't need it anymore. *Amen.*

Growth

GOD, we sit next to a glass of cool water, and we live our lives thirsty and dry. We stand just outside the shade, complain about the heat—when all we need is in front of us. All we need is within our reach, and we ignore it. Sometimes it's easier to complain than receive what you freely offer us. Help us take our minds off ourselves, God. Help us focus on you, and then we will see that you've already given us everything we need. Open our eyes to the world around us, and we will see that the missing pieces to our puzzle were right in front of us all along. Complete us, God. *Amen.*

FATHER, when is our time coming? We wait at your door. We listen at your feet, and still we feel like we're standing alone. The world is falling apart. The oceans are filling with filth, the sky is burning up, and your children are killing each other. We wait, God. We wait because your son told us to wait. Jesus said we would grieve and then find joy. But joy seems a long way off, God. If you would show us just a moment, just a glimpse, just a hint of the joy, love, laughter, and beauty you have for us, we could get through another day. We could survive these troubled times. We could go on listening and waiting until your kingdom comes. Give us a hint, God. *Amen.*

Guidance

GOD, there's a reason the Bible and the hymnals call you shepherd and us sheep. We get lost easily. We wander away without thinking. We follow the path with the greener grass, even if it takes us away from you. Sheep are born followers. What one does, they all do. We follow the ones with the most money or the loudest voices or coolest clothes, and we think we're on the path to happiness. You are the shepherd. You bring us back to the path even though we know it isn't the easiest way to go. We get lost, and you will leave the flock and come and find us again and again. You know us better than anyone. We know that all we must do is listen for your voice and follow your call. Watch over us, God. Keep us on the path. Amen

GOD, your work is not easy, but then again, you never said it would be. Too often we're too haggard and grumpy to get out of bed in the morning, let alone rejoice in the day you gave us. It's hard to remember that the drivers who cut us off are also your children. Open our eyes, God. We walk through this life in a fog and don't see what's around us. Help us remember that if we just give up our self-centered desires, you'll give us all we need—and more. Help us give our hearts and hands to your use, then we'll watch you bless us beyond our wildest imaginations. Faith comes in small steps, God. Point us in the right direction...again. Show us the path...again. Light our way with your Word...again. This time we will listen. This time we will walk. But God, don't go too far away. We may need you down the road. *Amen.*

GOD, long before you hung the stars in the sky, you knew what kind of day we'll have tomorrow. Before you created the mountains, you knew what we would become. Like a parent watching a child taking his first steps, you watched over us and held our hands and picked us up when we fell. And when we walked so far off the path that we couldn't hear your call, you sent your son. Through Jesus we learned about your plan. Through Jesus we found a home. Through Jesus we're signed, sealed, and delivered to you. Through Jesus we learned that all of this is only the beginning. *Amen.*

GOD, we've seen your work in our lives. We've felt what it's like to be down so low beneath the waves that we can't see the surface of the ocean. But you've lifted us from the well. You've been right beside us all this time. You've listened to us grumble about silly, trivial things, and you've never left our side. We ask you for so much, and you ask us for so little. All our needs have been met, and all you ask is belief in you. Yet we drive around in circles looking for you even though you know the way. God help us learn...really learn. Help us open our ears and truly listen. We've seen with our eyes and heard with our ears, and now we want you to help us believe with all our hearts. We want to stop complaining and instead focus on Jesus. Let us hear his words. Let us believe his truth and live in his love. *Amen.*

GOD, we are on the path. Though it seems we may be alone at times, we know we're on the right path. Your words light our way in the darkness and guide us like the stars. Your truth corrects us, encourages us, binds us, and lifts us up. We are believers in the Word; therefore we are all teachers of the Word. And we are all students. We are all encouragers. We are all lights. Help us to show the world your love. The world is a thirsty place right now, God. The eyes and throats of your children are caked with dust. Help us give them relief, God. Help us give them rest. Transform us into cool water and pour us all over your tired, thirsty children so that the world may see your love through us. Even to those who mock us and hate us. Giving your love to the world is like trying to empty the ocean with a spoon: There's way more of your love than we can imagine. Let us bring your water to the world. Those who walk in the desert will listen. And they will drink. *Amen.*

Hard Times

GOD, sometimes it just doesn't make sense. We live in a world that says, "Look out for number one," and yet you tell us to think of others. The world tells us to buy more, and you tell us to give it away. Following you makes us foolish in the world's eyes. But it's not the world's opinion that we care about. To the world we are weak, but in your eyes we are strong. There is joy in our obedience to you. If we follow your path, you'll be there at the end of it. If we stray from the path, we'll get caught in the briar and brambles. And when we find our way back to you, we're bruised, tired, and hungry. Then we wonder what was so important that we left the path for it in the first place. Help us keep our eyes on our destination. Light your heavenly home so that we won't be distracted by something shiny off the beaten path. *Amen.*

Holy Week

FATHER GOD, Palm Sunday is the tap of the first domino in the line. It's the moment before the stone enters the water. Today is the top of the first roller coaster hill. We are strapped in, and we can only ride it out to the end. Give us the faith to throw our hands in the air and cheer! Give us the courage to open our eyes and see it all—the beauty and the pain. After all, the same crowd that cheered your son's arrival screamed for his execution a few days later. Father, help us be the disciples and not the crowd. Give us just the smallest hint of who you are and what we can become through you, and we will follow you to the end of it. *Amen.*

FATHER GOD, we hear the sound of thirty pieces of silver rattling around, and we're shocked that the sound is coming from our own pockets. If we seek those who betray Christ, we need not look any further than in our church and in our mirror. The lessons are written down for us. The words of Christ are posted on flashing neon signs, so bright we can't ignore them. Then we turn around, and our actions put us to shame. Still, Jesus came back and forgave those who turned their backs on him. Right now we cling to the promise that he's doing the same for us. Want to feel the loving hands of Christ on our shoulders. We want to look into his eyes and be forgiven for many ways we mess up our lives. Forgive us God for all the stupid things we've done and all the stupid things we're going to do. *Amen.*

GOD, we don't wait very well. We are impatient. We don't like to wait in line. We don't like to wait for our computers to download files. We want things done in our time. Help us remember that Jesus knew that his time was nearly over. While we selfishly demand that things move faster, Jesus was praying for time to slow down. All things are done in your time, God. Help us put our lives into the hands of the one whose hands were nailed to the cross. Things will come to us as they come to us. Your will, not ours, God. *Amen.*

Homework

GOD, what moron came up with the concept of homework? Half the time it's just busy work. Half the time it's the things our teachers didn't plan well enough to say in class. Why do they do this? We're so bogged down. If we fell into the pool with all the home- work we have, it would pull us to the bottom. Is this "wealth of knowledge" really some- thing we need? Is the world we're to inherit really so bloodthirsty that it has to teach how to stay awake half the night doing math problems or writing essays? We have a lot of fears, God. Homework is just a mild irritation compared to some of the things we have to go through. You are the creator of the universe. You are the beginning and the end. Could you just give us a small hint of what we could be, so that we can keep going? Enrich us. Support us. Renew us. Give us a light in the distance so we can keep slogging through his mud. *Amen.*

Hope

FATHER, you display your existence to us every day, and still we sit back and wonder where you are. Miracles happen under our very noses, and we still don't see them. We make our way through life as if we walked into the wrong classroom and had to stay for the lecture. We don't pay attention. Still you surround us. You show us your love. But we've been in this rut for so long that we take everything for granted. Help us snap out of it, God. Open our minds so we can have the pure faith of children. Keep us from being skeptical and cynical. Your love is before us. It's in the rain, the sun, the Scriptures, and in the faces of those around us. Reach down and pull us out of the ditch we've dug for our- selves. We are your children, Lord. *Amen.*

Independence Day

FATHER GOD, the sounds of firecrackers and bottle rockets are more than a celebration of our country's independence. They are reminders of those who died for our freedom. Many have fallen around the world so that we can have the chance to celebrate on this day. So during the picnics let us remember those who're still serving far away. Let us remember the freedoms that we have and take for granted. We have the freedom to worship you, praise you, thank you for the gifts you have given us. We wouldn't be so blessed if it weren't for the men and women who've made the ultimate sacrifice to give us this freedom. We thank you, God, for the gift of the brave men and women who died protecting our freedoms and those who protect us now. *Amen.*

Justice

LORD, we think about justice more than we're given credit for. Killers and rapists walk free. Business tycoons who steal millions spend a few months in a country club. We hear people say, "There is no justice anymore!" Is that true, God? Our leaders have given us the right to punish the guilty and free the innocent, but it still seems all screwed up, God. Where's the justice for the kid who gets beaten up on the playground? Where's the justice for the fast-food worker who gets abused by an angry customer? Where are you in all of this, God? We know those who lose will gain in heaven. We know those who are abused will be admired. We know the hungry will be fed. Help us to provide those things now. Help us to feed the hungry. Help us to stand up for those who have no rights. Help us to bring justice for those that need it in this life. *Amen.*

Judging Others

GOD, one of the hardest things to learn is that we're all your children. Your Word is a light on our path and still we make our own rules about who can walk with us. We decide who can sit where. We make rules about who can worship and who can't. We cater to the rich and the pretty. We decide who's guilty without the evidence. We have a tendency to follow the rules we like and ignore the rules we don't. Don't judge us, God. Don't treat us the way we treat others, even though we deserve it. Help us instead. Mercy will win over harsh judgment. Help us be merciful. Help us to live our lives as people who will be judged by how we treat others. The mercy we receive will be equal to the mercy we give. Our clothes, cars, offices, and treasures will not count for much in the end. Each day is a new chance to show our love to you by showing love to all your children. *Amen.*

Lock-Ins

FATHER GOD, just as we're locked in this building tonight, we sometimes shut off ourselves from you. We hide. We assume that if we put up walls that you can't come in. We forget that you are with us always. We forget that you are in our hearts. You know us so well that we can't ever be away from you. You surround us. You support us from beneath our feet and watch over us from above. If we go to the top of the highest mountain, you are there. If we journey to the farthest point on the earth, you are there to lead us home. Forgive us, God, for our fears and our hiding. Help us to understand you so that we can truly love you. Help us to never want to be away from your love. Amen

CREATOR OF THE NIGHT SKY, we gather in this place to worship you. For now, all that could harm us or worry us is locked out. We feel safe—until we remember that tomorrow we must leave this sanctuary and be part of the crazy world again. We take comfort in knowing that when we leave this place, you will be with us. You will hold our hands like a loving parent and walk with us. You will guide our feet. When we face those things that vex us or scare us, you will be beside us. Sometimes when we lock ourselves in, we forget that along with those things we fear, the world is also full of things we love. Help us take the feelings of love and safety with us when we leave tomorrow. We know you are there for us, God. *Amen.*

IT'S QUIET IN OUR CHURCH, GOD. When the boom box is turned down and the games are over, there's a silence about your house that can be unnerving. Help us to listen to the quiet. We know you don't come to us in a storm or a fire but in a still, small voice. Help us to be quiet, Lord. Help us to listen for that quiet voice. Help us to feel that gentle breeze that blows past our faces and know you are here. You are speaking to us. Help us to be open to your words, God. Even though it may not always look like it...we are listening. *Amen.*

Loving Our Enemies

GOD, our faith isn't supposed to get us in trouble. We follow your ways. We listen to your words. We pray to you, sing to you, and there are those who hate us because of it. How can people possibly hate your music? How can people possibly hate the sound of your name? There are times, God, when it seems like it would be better if we just kept our mouths shut. But we are your children, and we cannot keep quiet about that. You are the creator of the universe, and you have promised us a reward beyond our imaginations. Until the day when you welcome us into your arms, we will settle for your reassuring hand on our shoulders. *Amen.*

Masks

GOD, the most frightening part of being one of your children is that it's so easy to fake. There are days when we don't want to be happy-go-lucky Christians. There are days when we hurt inside. There are days when our faith is weak. We hide our faces behind masks that show the world we are yours—but behind the false veil we are weeping. Give us the courage to remove our masks, God. Give us the guts to show the world we can hurt, too. We believe in your son, Jesus. But our masks won't lead others to him. We can only point the way to Jesus as one beggar shows another where the food is. Unveil us God. *Amen.*

Miracles

GOD, we can do miracles. The world looks at us and says, "Where is your God when so many are hungry? Your God doesn't care!" The world is wrong. We know you love us, God. Why? Because you gave us hands to make bread—so the hungry can eat. Because you gave us the skill to build houses—so homeless people can stay warm and dry. Because you gave us each other—so we wouldn't be lonely. We can show the world exactly where you are, God. You live in our world because you live in us! We won't wait for the hungry, homeless, and lonely come to us for help—we will go find them. Just as you did, Lord. Thank you for coming to earth and finding us. *Amen.*

Missions (General)

GOD, you call us to follow your son. You call us to feed your lambs and take care of your sheep, and we feel hopelessly unqualified. You ask us again and again, and we make the promise and still let you down. God, your son stretched out his arms and died so that we might know your love. We desperately want to please you. Like Peter we have failed you, and you have every right to call our sincerity into question. But our mistakes make us stronger, God. We learn hard lessons, and we grow more determined. Your lambs are hungry, they are cold, and they are lost. We will find them, feed them, and shelter them. We will do all of these things because you asked us to, God. We are your servants. *Amen.*

GOD, your children are hungry. They're lonely. They're cold. Don't let us walk by them on the other side of the road, God. We get so caught up in our own lives and our own so-called "problems" that we forget there are people who sleep in the streets. Open our eyes. Light a fire under us so that we can do all Jesus told us we should do. Help us give a hand up and not a hand out. Help us show the world we are your children. Help us show the world that the church is more than building with brick and stained glass. Church is a warm blanket, a hot meal, a listening ear. When we offer ourselves to those in need, Lord, we offer ourselves to you. *Amen.*

Mission Week Prayers

Day One

LORD, we are ready. We are here in this place to be your servants. We all desperately want to please you, both those of us who've done this before and those of us who're brand new at it. We enter this week looking to receive nothing in return. We expect nothing from those we'll serve. Your son taught us to love without condition. We will show the world that kind of love this week, Lord. We will work with each other side by side. We will put away our differences and do your will. We are energized, Lord! We can't wait to begin! Pace us, though, Father. Help us keep this feeling the entire week. Keep our hearts and minds on the work before us. We know we are the only "Jesus" that some of these people will ever see. Help us to show them the true Christ. The Son of God. Help us to show the unconditional love of our Savior. With your help we can. *Amen.*

Midweek

WE ARE GROWING WEARY, LORD. Our hands hurt. Our feet ache. More than once we've asked ourselves, "Why are we doing this?" Then we remember. We see the faces of those we serve. We see our accomplishments. We see the roads we've begun to journey down, and we remember why we do this. Give us strength, Lord. Our hearts are willing—but our bodies need help! But we want you to strengthen our resolve—not just our bodies. Strengthen our hearts…and our hands will follow. Let us feel your love, and the rest will be easy. Your servants will not fail you. We are of one mind and heart. We are here to do your work. We are here to spread your love and your word. Give us rest and peace of mind. Let us put away those things that distract us from the job at hand. Help us remember that we are here in the name of your son, Jesus Christ our Lord. *Amen.*

End of week

GOD, we're still here! We survived. We are your servants. We have accomplished so much with our hands and hearts. We have shown the world that you are who you say you are, the giver of everlasting love. We take pride in what we've done. And we have done well. Now it's time for us to go home and rest—a well-deserved rest. But as we go home to "real" lives, help us to remember that our "real" lives are alien to the people we've served here. Help us to better appreciate what we have at home. Help us to remember the faces of your children who don't have the good things we have. Help us to walk in your love for the rest of our lives as we have walked in your love this week. *Amen.*

New Year's Eve

FATHER IN HEAVEN, we are coming to a close. The old year is ending. Help us let it go, Lord. Help us to not look back and long for it. Help us keep our eyes facing forward. Help us to see the new. The problems and difficulties we had last year are gone. We step into this New Year not alone, but with you. We need your hand to guide us, your eyes to watch over us, and your Word to light our paths. Each New Year is a journey. Help us make the first step. Let us wait patiently and then begin a new life as the New Year begins. *Amen.*

GOD, as the second hand passes 12, we know it means more than the passing of another second. It's the passing of a year. And there is some shame in each one of us. We recall the things we did and said that we wish we could change. Thank you for your forgiveness, Lord. And help us start this New Year knowing our sins are behind us. Help us forgive those who've wronged us. And forgive us as we forgive others. *Amen.*

New Year's Day

GOD, you have placed a new path in front of us. We've celebrated the coming of this New Year—now let us begin it well! Let us step into it knowing that we are walking it with you. The old is behind us. Everything you want us to be is in front of us. You have given us yet another chance to please you, to walk with you, to be your children. God, it's so hard to not look back. Keep our eyes on the horizon, Lord. There's so much we can be. There's so much we can achieve. There's so much in front of us that we can hardly wait to get started. Help us leave behind the fears that can hold us back. Stay with us as we begin this journey. *Amen.*

Open Our Eyes

GOD, your power and presence are all around us. You're in the sunshine at the beginning of each new day—and in the stars we see at night. We want to see your miracles. We want to feel the presence of the Holy Spirit. We go through life wearing blinders and headphones, unaware that we're in the presence of the Creator of the universe. So when we have one of those days where everything we touch falls apart, open our eyes to you. When we have arguments with friends, family members, and coworkers, show us that you're there for us then, too. Lord, you call us by name. You show us your miracles every day. Open our eyes God. We will see. Call us again. We will listen. *Amen.*

Patience

CREATOR GOD, we get frustrated so much. And then we say things in your presence that we'd never utter in front of our children. Because we love Jesus, help us to be courteous to each other. Out of respect for Christ, we won't yell at the teenager working the drive-thru. Out of respect for Christ, we will smile and say hello to the tollbooth attendant. Out of respect for Christ, we won't get impatient with the fast-lane drivers going 20 miles an hour below the speed limit. Help us get through this week with songs on our lips, God. Help us make music with our hearts and remember to thank you for each new day. Help us to thank you for the rain. Help us to thank you for sunshine. Help us to thank you for the cool breeze that blows across our skin when we do yard work. We are grateful, God. Help us to show it to you and to the world. *Amen.*

Peace

GOD, praying for peace is like asking to be fed when the food is right in front of us. We can create peace ourselves—but we are afraid. We are afraid we will lose. We are afraid to look stupid. We are afraid of what others will think. Peace comes from being in the right place at the right time. Lead us to that place, God. Lead us to a place where we don't have to fight or argue anymore. Lead us to a place where we are no longer afraid. We will listen. We will wait. Just don't let us wait too long, God. It's scary out here. *Amen.*

Praise God

GOD, we are your children. If only the rest of the world could know what an amazing idea that is! We are the creations of the ultimate Creator! We are the loved ones of a power so far beyond our comprehension that we can't begin to understand it ourselves. But we have faith. We have the faith that if we live by the light of your Word, then we will see Jesus. It's easy to get confused, God. It's easy to get it all backward. It's not enough to know the way you want us to live. We must be able to live that way. God, help us not to be lead astray by people with more toys than us. Help us to live right. And in living right, we shall be right with you. Because we shall be your children. *Amen.*

FATHER, forgive us. In our efforts to understand you, we have made you small. We have tried to make you like us instead of the other way around. In wanting to see your face, we create images that look like us instead of you. In wanting to hear your voice, we listen to music full of messages we didn't understand in the first place. Help us to look for you in our hearts, Lord, and not on the television or the stereo or the computer. We will see your creation, and we will be filled. We will rejoice in your name. *Amen.*

Protection

GOD, we wouldn't go into the pouring rain without an umbrella. We wouldn't stand on a blazing beach in the afternoon without sun block. Don't let us go into this world without your Word. Truth, righteousness, peace, faith, and salvation are more than words. They are our protection in this world. We will carry them all our lives. Help us to learn them well. Our daily lives here shouldn't be taken lightly. Each day we venture out, we must be prepared. Help us to teach your Word to our children. Better yet, help us to live your Word so that our children may learn from us. We will pray long and hard. We will pray for our families and friends. We will pray for our leaders and our world. We will live each day honored to be children of God.

The Rain

THERE IS NO SOUND LIKE RAIN, GOD. Rain on a roof, rain on the ground, rain on the trees, it's all good. There is a sense of newness in the water, God. There is a sense of second chances. You send the rain to care for the planet. It brings new life and new hope. The rain brings relief. We need these things, too, God. We need new life. We need hope. God, we need relief! But there is joy in the water. There is joy in the drenching feeling of playing in the rain. There is peace in the sound and smell of it. Wash away all that covers us, God. Our mistakes cling to us like dirt. Make us new, God. Thank you for this rain. Thank you for second chances. Thank you for the newness of life around us. Thank you for the sound of the rain, God. *Amen.*

Self-Image

GOD, give us faith in ourselves. When the supermodels are too skinny, help us love ourselves. When the ballplayers make millions for a few free throws, help us to be thankful for the ability to breathe! You placed each star in the sky exactly where it needs to be. You placed people on this earth where you wanted on them. We are at the right place at the right time. Please open our minds so we can understand what you want from us, God. We are your servants. We will go where you send. Help us not to grumble about who's in line ahead of us. Our place in line doesn't matter one bit—because we're all part of the big picture. You are the artist. As each ingredient in the recipe works with the others, so must we work to create a world worthy of your continued presence. *Amen.*

Selfishness

GOD, we spend too much time asking, "What's in it for me?" We call ourselves your children and sing your praises, and then we ignore those in need and walk away from the sick and the hurting. Help us get our priorities in order, God. Help us put you first, others second, and ourselves third. The world may laugh at us, God. It may not understand. The world tells us to look out for number one, but you tell us to look out for each other. We refuse to let others feel lonely. We will pay attention to those around us and offer a hand or a shoulder or an ear. We know that when we look after each other, we are looking after your son, our savior, Jesus Christ. *Amen.*

FATHER, we love our "things." We want more "things." We don't understand how we could possibly be happy without our things. What if we lost all our possessions? What if everything we owned was taken from us? Could we still be happy? Would we blame you, God? Our time on this earth is so limited. The time we spend with family and friends can be over before we're ready. Each day is a gift, God. Open our eyes and hearts and help us appreciate every minute you offer us. Help us to appreciate the smell of coffee. Help us to see the rain as a gift and the sunrise as your creation. Help us ready our hearts and minds for your call. Help us make sure our souls are in order—instead of our houses. The piles of things we accumulate won't mean anything when you open your arms and call us home. Help us to appreciate the important things in this life you've given us—and long before we spend our eternity with you. *Amen.*

Small Hours of the Night

GOD, there's something about this time of night. There's a mystery to it we want to understand. Around us people sleep and dream. The darkness can make us feel like we're walking through someone else's dream. All those things that are present in the light are still here in the dark. But the darkness can be cold, Lord. Please wrap your arms around us! Hold us like a parent holds a child in the darkness of the night. Make us feel safe and warm. Carry us. We are just babies. Walk back and forth across the room while you sing softly to us. Bring us comfort, Lord. Take our worries and fears away and hold us until morning comes. *Amen.*

FATHER, sometimes it seems like time stands still. In the small hours of the night, it's as though time slows down, and we pass through the dark, unhampered by the ticking of the clock. God, you are the beginning and the end. You are a creator so far beyond our understanding that we can't hope to learn all there is to know about you. An eternity would not be enough time. But for some reason you wait for us, Lord. You have so much patience. We get lost time and time again, yet over and over you lead us back home. Lord, in the quiet of this night, lead us back to the right path again. Hold our hands and walk with us until the sun comes up. *Amen.*

Sunrise—New Day—Second Chances

GOD, make us as the sun. Let the light of your love shine through us. Let your joy shoot from our bodies so we are shining. Let us take your love into a world of darkness. There are so many people out there who are lost and waiting for someone to light the way. On this new day, make us your servants, God. Let people look to us for light. The sun shines on everybody, Lord. Anyone can stand in its warmth and see by its light. Make us like the sun, God. Help us to be worthy of the job. When people look to us, let us show them the light of your love. Let us light the path so that they can find you, too. *Amen.*

GOD, thank you for bringing the sun up slowly. I don't think our brains could take the blast if it all lit up at once. God, we know you reveal yourself to us slowly. We want so badly to know you, but you are the one who knows better. You know we couldn't take it all at once. Like the sun illuminates the world around us slowly, so you illuminate our lives. We grow to see ourselves and understand ourselves because you let us learn a little at time. You are a God of small doses. Keep teaching us, Lord. Understand our enthusiasm and our denials. We are searching in the dark too much. Show us your love, God. Illuminate our lives just a little more each day. Light our world so that we can find our way back to you. *Amen.*

Sunset—Peace of Mind—Worries

GOD, we stand here amazed by you. When we stop to take it all in, we can't help being amazed. Everything we've seen, everything we've heard—everything is because of you. The wind, the rain, the stars in the night sky—they're all your doing. Yet everything that has happened has happened because of you. We know you take all things, both good and bad, and make them work for you. You can take everything that happens and make it good. It has been a full day, Lord. As this night begins, let us take stock of our lives. Help us to open our minds and hearts to your wisdom. Keep amazing us, God. *Amen.*

THE DAY IS DONE, GOD. We've done enough. Center us now. Calm our minds. Help us put all the pettiness aside. The day is done. It is in the past. All the things that bothered us today are no more. If we were hurt, help us give the pain to you. If we were wronged, help us give the anger to you. If we hurt or wronged someone else, forgive us—and help us ask that someone else for forgiveness. When the sun sets, we put it all behind us. We can't dwell in the past. Jesus is a light to our path, but the path only goes forward. Keep us walking in the right direction, God. Walk with us. Show us the way. *Amen.*

Thanksgiving

GOD, all things come from you. There is nothing that happens in our lives without your knowing. We have so much, God. We take it all for granted. The sun comes up in the morning. The ocean rolls into the shore. The stars shine. The leaves change color. Thank you, God, for these gifts. Thank you for the people who love us in spite of ourselves. Thank you for your son who was nailed to the cross. Thank you for the independence and perseverance of our forefathers who saw beyond their own existences and created this nation. *Amen.*

Unity

FATHER GOD, even the disciples must have been confused. Your son died. He rose again. And the disciples had to ask, "Now what?" We sit like the followers, God. We wait. Like children we wait to be told what to do next. Please send Jesus into our house, Lord. Send him into our hearts. Unite us in the message and the mission, God. Show us the way, and we will go. Unite us in the spirit, and we will believe. Unite us in your love, and we will love. We aren't the only ones praying, either. Across the city, the state, the country, and the world, others are praying, too. Bind us together, Lord. Let us live as one. *Amen.*

Valentine's Day

GOD, this is a day of hearts and candy. Of love notes and secret messages, new discoveries, and new emotions. It's a day all about love. But help us to remember that you love us as your children. You love us without condition. Help us understand that we could not celebrate on this day of "love" if you had not first loved us! We wouldn't know what love is if you hadn't first loved us. While we thank you for chocolate, roses, and funny sayings on candy hearts, help us to remember that these expressions are temporal—on some Valentine's Days we'll have them…and on others we won't. They're all possible because of you, Lord. *Amen.*

Weekends

KEEP US SAFE, GOD. We've spent a week feeling like we walk around in leg irons, and now we're free. Prevent us from getting stupid. And keep us safe if we get stupid, Lord. We thank you for this emotional break from the world. School can seem like a deep well, God. The waters are always rising. We learn to stay ahead, just for a few days, but soon the waters threaten to rise up and drown us. Thank you for this break, God. Thank you for allowing us to relax and enjoy the cool of the water without struggling against it. Thank you for the time to breathe, to laugh, and to rejuvenate our minds. *Amen.*

IN LOVING MEMORY OF JAMES PIERCE WITHERS 18__-192_ · A FAITHFUL AND DEVOTED COMMUNICANT OF THIS CHURCH

Responsive Readings

When you use the section, tell the group that this is a responsive reading, and they are supposed to say the response in **bold** after each statement you make. These readings are perfect for getting your teenagers involved in the service. They are categorized by topics broad enough so that they can be used with multiple services.

Acceptance / Getting Along

Lord, let us remember we're all your children

Lord, lets us be as one.

Let us remember we're all made in your image

Lord, lets us be as one.

Lord, when we can't agree

Lord, let us be as one.

When we can't get along

Lord, let us be as one.

When the little things irritate us

Lord, let us be as one.

When we come to you

Lord, let us bc as one.

When we sing

Lord, let us be as one.

When we pray

Lord, let us be as one.

Help us to support each other

Lord, let us be as one.

Help us to lift each other up

Lord, let us be as one.

Help us to look around and appreciate the differences and then

Lord, let us be as one.

In your sight.

Amen.

Acceptance/Racism

God, you've given us this earth

Because we are all your children.

You've given us each other

Because we are all your children.

You've given us our families

Because we are all your children.

God, help us to learn

Because we are all your children.

Help us understand that the color of skin doesn't matter

Because we are all your children.

Help us understand that where we come from does not matter

Because we are all your children.

Help us know that you want us to love each other

Because we are all your children.

Help us celebrate our differences

Because we are all your children.

And gather together in your sight to worship you together

Because we are all your children.

Amen.

Accepting Ourselves

We are not supermodels or professional athletes.

God does not make mistakes.

We are the children of God.

God does not make mistakes.

God has a plan.

God does not make mistakes.

He may not share it with you all at once.

God does not make mistakes.

But God has a plan.

God does not make mistakes.

God sees the whole puzzle.

God does not make mistakes.

We only see one small piece.

God does not make mistakes.

We will believe.

God does not make mistakes.

We will take comfort in the promise that God is the potter

God does not make mistakes.

We are the clay.

God does not make mistakes.

Amen.

Belief

The world may say otherwise.

There is one God.

Some will worship money.

There is one God.

Some will worship power.

There is one God.

Some will worship material things.

There is one God.

The ancients had a separate god for everything.

There is one God.

Some believed in worshiping idols.

There is one God.

God said it to Moses.

There is one God.

Jesus said to his followers.

There is one God.

We will say it to the world.

There is one God.

Father of all

There is one God.

Creator of the universe

There is one God.

Friend and companion

There is one God.

Redeemer and inspiration

There is one God.

Who always was

There is one God.

Who is now

There is one God.

Who always will be

There is one God.

Now and forever

There is one God.

Amen.

Belief

God was there for Daniel.

God is here.

God was there for Joseph.

God is here.

God was there for Jesus.

God is here.

God was there for Paul.

God is here.

We all have our own problems.

God is here.

We all feel alone sometimes.

God is here.

When I am on the mountaintop

God is here.

When I am in a valley of despair

God is here.

When I don't even think about it

God is here.

I am not alone.

God is here.

I will never be alone.

God is here.

I am loved.

God is here.

With a love that's beyond measure.

God is here.

Without condition.

God is here.

I am loved.

God is here.

I am not alone.

God is here.

God is now and forever.

God is here.

I don't have to worry.

God is here.

Amen.

Body of Christ

We are the work of the Creator.

We are the body of Christ.

We all have a place.

We are the body of Christ.

Heads for thinking.

We are the body of Christ.

Hands for working.

We are the body of Christ.

Feet for walking.

We are the body of Christ.

Hearts for loving.

We are the body of Christ.

Shoulders for carrying.

We are the body of Christ.

Ears for listening.

We are the body of Christ.

Mouths for praising.

We are the body of Christ.

Eyes for watching.

We are the body of Christ.

We are Christ's hands in this world.

We are the body of Christ.

What he started we will continue.

We are the body of Christ.

Christ is alive in this world.

We are the body of Christ.

He lives in us.

We are the body of Christ.

Amen.

Christmas Hope

In the eyes of a small child lying awake
in bed on Christmas Eve.

Lord, we see the hope

in the eyes of a woman seeing her 90th
Christmas.

Lord, we see the hope

in the memories of a man spending his
first Christmas alone.

Lord, we see the hope

in the lights on the tree and the lights in
the night sky.

Lord, we see the hope

in the present that rattles when you
shake it.

Lord, we see the hope

in the cookbook of holiday recipes.

Lord, we see the hope

in the praise of the teacher helping the
troubled student.

Lord, we see the hope

in the glowing star at the top of the tree.

Lord, we see the hope

in the star that led the wise men to the
Christ child.

Lord, we see the hope

in the arms of the mother holding her
first newborn.

Lord, we see the hope

in the heart of Mary holding the baby
Jesus.

Lord, we see the hope

Amen.

Christmas Faith

Father God, as the season gets hectic,
as our lives get crazy

Lord, give us the faith

to remember that the person who took
our parking spot is also your child.

Lord, give us the faith

to understand that seasonal employees
are only temporary.

Lord, give us the faith

to believe that our change in the
Salvation Army pot does make a
difference.

Lord, give us the faith

to remember that having all the family
coming to our house is a good thing.

Lord, give us the faith

in ourselves that we can somehow stay
focused on our schoolwork.

Lord, give us the faith

in each other to believe that we can all
praise you and worship you without
expectation.

Lord, give us the faith

to pray and believe that we are heard.

Lord, give us the faith

to pray for those who don't have
blankets—not for gifts we think we
need.

Lord, give us the faith

of a child who sees decorating the
Christmas tree as a gift and not a chore.

Lord, give us the faith

of the child who sees the world through
eyes filled with wonder.

Lord, give us the faith

to believe this candle is but one light
among a million others that will guide
your children to back to you.

Amen.

Christmas Joy

Joy to the world.

JOY!!

to the woman working in the complaint department.

JOY!!

to the kid working the drive-thru at the fast-food joint.

JOY!!

to the postal workers, waitresses, and teachers.

JOY!!

to children trying to stay focused in school.

JOY!!

to people whose Christmas dinner will be eaten on a paper plate with a plastic fork.

JOY!!

to those who spend the holiday in the kitchen.

JOY!!

to those who spend the holiday in the hospital.

JOY!!

to those who spend the holiday alone.

JOY!!

to the world.

Amen.

Christmas Peace

In troubled minds and troubled hearts

Lord, grant us peace.

In the times when we worry about what's on the store shelves

Lord, grant us peace.

When we worry about how many Christmas cards we received

Lord, grant us peace.

When we worry that the turkey is undercooked and the pie is burned

Lord, grant us peace.

When we remember the credit card statements

Lord, grant us peace.

When we remember how lucky we are

Lord, grant us peace.

When we give our change to beggars on the street

Lord, grant us peace.

When we give our thoughts to you in prayer

Lord, grant us peace.

So that we'll understand we are all your children

Lord, grant us peace.

So that we may give it to the homeless

Lord, grant us peace.

So that we may share it with our families and friends

Lord, grant us peace.

Amen.

Decisions about the Future

When we look into horizon and try to picture where we want to go

God is beside us on the path.

We are not alone, and though it sometimes feels that way

God is beside us on the path.

When we have dreams and nightmares about where we'll end up

God is beside us on the path.

When we've been given so much advice that we wind up even more confused.

God is beside us on the path.

When we want the right school and the right job

God is beside us on the path.

When we have enough money

God is beside us on the path.

When we have to remember

God is beside us on the path.

He will walk with us.

God is beside us on the path.

He will carry us when we are tired.

God is beside us on the path.

We are servants of God.

God is beside us on the path.

God will never put us someplace that we cannot handle.

God is beside us on the path.

God would never have us make this decision alone.

God is beside us on the path.

All things are possible

God is beside us on the path.

Amen.

Deciding to Follow God

How can you believe in a God who doesn't seem to listen?

I decided to.

How can you believe in a virgin birth?

I decided to.

How can you believe the meek will be blessed?

I decided to.

How can you believe that good wins when the bad guys always seem to?

I decided to.

How can you believe in a heaven you can't see?

I decided to.

How can you believe in a savior you've never met?

I decided to.

How can you study a book that was written centuries ago?

I decided to.

How can you help people who don't help themselves?

I decided to.

How can you love your enemies?

I decided to.

How can you keep praying when you never get what you want?

I decided to.

How can you believe blindly that there's a purpose for your life?

I decided to.

How can you keep loving the unbelievers?

I decided to.

If I asked God why he loves you, what would he say?

I decided to.

Amen.

Discipleship

God looked down and saw his people hurting.

I will follow the carpenter.

He sent prophets and preachers.

I will follow the carpenter.

Finally he sent his son.

I will follow the carpenter.

Born as one of us

I will follow the carpenter.

He called the disciples.

I will follow the carpenter.

He calls us.

I will follow the carpenter.

He suffered under a cruel king.

I will follow the carpenter.

He was arrested and murdered.

I will follow the carpenter.

He came back.

I will follow the carpenter.

He came back.

I will follow the carpenter.

He message is simple.

I will follow the carpenter.

Love God.

I will follow the carpenter.

Love God with all your heart mind and soul.

I will follow the carpenter.

Love each other.

I will follow the carpenter.

Easy to hear. Hard to do.

I will follow the carpenter.

We will.

I will follow the carpenter.

We were called to do so.

I will follow the carpenter.

Nothing can hold us back.

I will follow the carpenter.

Amen.

Easter

The disciples saw him arrested, beaten, and die.

Jesus came back!

They saw him wrapped in rags and placed in a grave.

Jesus came back!

His enemies said, "There! That should take care of that!"

Jesus came back!

Centuries of leaders have tried to say he was never real.

Jesus came back!

Centuries of leaders have tried to put him in a box.

Jesus came back!

They tried to limit him.

Jesus came back!

They tried to dilute him.

Jesus came back!

They tried to drown him out.

Jesus came back!

We, too, have pushed him away.

Jesus came back!

In our actions and words, we have betrayed him.

Jesus came back!

We have screamed at him in anger.

Jesus came back!

We have used his name in vain.

Jesus came back!

Time will not see him fade.

Jesus came back!

With the Father and the Holy Ghost, he will live forever.

Jesus came back!

Amen.

Enlightenment

God we've read your words.

God, we need to know you are there.

We've seen the video.

God, we need to know you are there.

We talk about faith.

God, we need to know you are there.

Our brains demand evidence.

God, we need to know you are there.

Our hearts long to believe.

God, we need to know you are there.

Forgive us our doubts, God.

God, we need to know you are there.

The world is a cruel place.

God, we need to know you are there.

The hungry and hurting reach out.

God, we need to know you are there.

The questions and doubts rise up on us like water.

God, we need to know you are there.

We could drown in our own ignorance.

God, we need to know you are there.

Come into this place.

God, we need to know you are there.

We will open our hardened hearts.

God, we need to know you are there.

We will open our minds and souls.

God, we need to know you are there.

Show us.

God, we need to know you are there.

Enlighten us.

God, we need to know you are there.

Amen.

Faith/Decisions

God, sometimes it feels like we spend a lot of time stumbling around in the dark.

Light the path, God.

There are so many choices.

Light the path, God.

So many people who want just a little piece our lives.

Light the path, God.

So many things that take up our time.

Light the path, God.

So many ways to mess up our lives.

Light the path, God.

We are not alone.

Light the path, God.

The dark is a scary place, but we are not alone.

Light the path, God.

You are with us God.

Light the path, God.

We may not know where we are going.

Light the path, God.

We can't see the end of the path.

Light the path, God.

We will trust you, God.

Light the path, God.

We will believe in your light.

Light the path, God.

Amen.

Faith

Father God, sometimes we feel
completely alone.
Joy comes in the morning.
We hear awful words and see horrible
things.
Joy comes in the morning.
There is too much to do.
Joy comes in the morning.
There is too little time.
Joy comes in the morning.
There is no one to help.
Joy comes in the morning.
It feels like everything I touch falls apart.
Joy comes in the morning.
Breaks down.
Joy comes in the morning.
Becomes worthless.
Joy comes in the morning.
But you are God.
Joy comes in the morning.
You know what we go through.
Joy comes in the morning.
You would never leave us alone.
Joy comes in the morning.
You are beside us when the world turns
bad.
Joy comes in the morning.
You are beside us when the world turns
its back on us.
Joy comes in the morning.
We need not worry.
Joy comes in the morning.
It's all good.
Joy comes in the morning.
It's all good.
Joy comes in the morning.
Amen.

Forgiveness

God, we have so much baggage.
Forgiveness isn't easy.
We say things we don't mean.
Forgiveness isn't easy.
We hang on to the pain like it's valuable.
Forgiveness isn't easy.
In the end it can only hurt us.
Forgiveness isn't easy.
It will weigh us down.
Forgiveness isn't easy.
Drag us under.
Forgiveness isn't easy.
You have forgiven us, God.
Forgiveness isn't easy.
For all the thoughts we don't say out
loud.
Forgiveness isn't easy.
For all those things we hope no one
knows.
Forgiveness isn't easy.
You ask us to forgive the ones who hurt
us
Forgiveness isn't easy.
As completely and easily as you forgive
us.
Forgiveness isn't easy.
Unconditionally.
Forgiveness isn't easy.
Without expecting anything in return.
Forgiveness isn't easy.
Help us to forgive them.
Forgiveness isn't easy.
Help us to forgive ourselves.
Forgiveness isn't easy.
Amen.

Forgiveness (ourselves)

God, we're here again.

Take us back, God.

We wandered off the path again.

Take us back, God.

Like we did the last time.

Take us back, God.

And the time before that.

Take us back, God.

Don't keep a record, God.

Take us back, God.

We know the way we're supposed to live.

Take us back, God.

Your son told us.

Take us back, God.

The Scriptures tell us.

Take us back, God.

Your servants tell us.

Take us back, God.

And we walk off the path anyway.

Take us back, God.

To follow something shiny.

Take us back, God.

To follow what we thought would be fun.

Take us back, God.

We will kneel down here in the dirt.

Take us back, God.

We will pray to you again.

Take us back, God.

Make us your servants.

Take us back, God.

Your servants will honor you.

Take us back, God.

Amen.

Forgiveness (others)

God, we have so much anger.

Help us let it go.

We hang onto it like a precious stone.

Help us let it go.

We keep it next to the pain.

Help us let it go.

We think we own it.

Help us let it go.

People hurt us, God.

Help us let it go.

People who mean well say things that hurt.

Help us let it go.

People who mean us harm seem to get such enjoyment out of it.

Help us let it go.

The pain will do us no good.

Help us let it go.

The anger will do us no good.

Help us let it go.

Why do we hold on to them so tightly?

Help us let it go.

Jesus forgave those who hated him.

Help us let it go.

He forgave those who drove nails through his hands.

Help us let it go.

He loved his enemies.

Help us let it go.

It hurts, God.

Help us let it go.

We are afraid.

Help us let it go.

Give us strength.

Help us let it go.

We will let it go.

Help us let it go.

We will let it go.

Help us let it go.

Help us God.

Help us let it go.

Amen.

Friendship

As you finish this reading, invite your students to shout out their own phrases for the others to respond to. Don't let it go overboard, though. Too many will take away from what's being said.

A good friend is hard to come by.

Make me a good friend, God.

A good friend will be there when you're down.

Make me a good friend, God.

A good friend will know you—and like you anyway.

Make me a good friend, God.

A friend will always share with you.

Make me a good friend, God.

A friend will always give you a kind word when you need it.

Make me a good friend, God.

A friend will make you laugh when you need it most.

Make me a good friend, God.

A friend will listen when you need to be heard.

Make me a good friend, God.

A friend will be honest with you no matter what.

Make me a good friend, God.

A friend will walk across a desert to give you a glass of water.

Make me a good friend, God.

A friend will share lunch when you forgot yours.

Make me a good friend, God.

A friend will never make you feel inferior.

Make me a good friend, God.

Add your own

Make me a good friend, God.

Add your own

Make me a good friend, God.

Add your own

Make me a good friend, God.

Add your own

Make me a good friend, God.

Amen.

Grace

Through the blood of Jesus the Christ

We receive the grace of God.

Through acts of charity and courage

We receive the grace of God.

Through acts of hope and kindness

We receive the grace of God.

By our knowledge

We receive the grace of God.

Our love

We receive the grace of God.

Our mercy

We receive the grace of God.

We gossip about our friends and still

We receive the grace of God.

We lose our patience with our family and yet

We receive the grace of God.

When we stand up after being beaten down

We receive the grace of God.

When we seek righteousness

We receive the grace of God.

When we make decisions based on the word of God

We receive the grace of God.

When we don't deserve it

We receive the grace of God.

Through the blood of our savior Jesus the Christ

We receive the grace of God.

Amen.

Growth

David took out the giant.

Give me room to grow.

Isaac was given a second chance.

Give me room to grow.

Joseph survived the well.

Give me room to grow.

Samuel heard his name called in the
night.

Give me room to grow.

Mary accepted the labor.

Give me room to grow.

Jesus endured the cross.

Give me room to grow.

The world wants us to stay down.

Give me room to grow.

We are sheltered from things it thinks
will harm us.

Give me room to grow.

We want to make our own mistakes.

Give me room to grow.

We want to live with the mistakes we
make.

Give me room to grow.

We are held back.

Give me room to grow.

We stand on the beach and look at the
horizon.

Give me room to grow.

We stand on the roof and look at the
stars.

Give me room to grow.

God will not leave us.

Give me room to grow.

God is not the destination.

Give me room to grow.

God is already with us on the way.

Give me room to grow.

If we listen with our ears and see with
our eyes

Give me room to grow.

And open our minds

Give me room to grow.

We will hear God.

Give me room to grow.

God will give us the room.

Give me room to grow.

Amen.

Guidance

God, sometimes we can't even find the
door.

Be our light on the path.

We stumble around in the dark.

Be our light on the path.

We lose our way.

Be our light on the path.

We can't see even where to put our feet.

Be our light on the path.

Let alone see the end of the journey.

Be our light on the path.

We will stop and take a deep breath.

Be our light on the path.

We will open our eyes to the
possibilities.

Be our light on the path.

We will pray for light.

Be our light on the path.

Show us the way, God.

Be our light on the path.

Calm our minds and soothe our souls.

Be our light on the path.

Show us the way, and we will go.

Be our light on the path.

Amen.

Love

God, the darkest night can still have hope
When there's love.
The coldest winter can still have warmth
When there's love.
Standing by ourselves we don't feel alone
When there's love.
Finding our way in the dark isn't as hard as we thought
When there's love.
There's help for the lost
When there's love.
There's a bed for the tired
When there's love.
There's food for the hungry
When there's love.
There's shelter for the homeless
When there's love.
There's relief for the sick
When there's love.
There's time together
When there's love.
We can accomplish anything
When there's love.
We can stop the fighting
When there's love.
We can hear the cries of the helpless
When there's love.
We find that one special person
When there's love.
We can choose the right path every time
When there's love.
We can be your children
When there's love.
Amen.

Obedience

God, we will stop fighting to get our own way.
God's law is alive.
We act like children being sent to our rooms.
God's law is alive.
Forgive our selfishness, God.
God's law is alive.
We will listen.
God's law is alive.
We will find the joy in obedience.
God's law is alive.
We will discover the reward in listening.
God's law is alive.
We will close our mouths and open our eyes.
God's law is alive.
You speak to us all the time.
God's law is alive.
We don't listen.
God's law is alive.
You show us right direction.
God's law is alive.
We turn the other way.
God's law is alive.
Show us how to live.
God's law is alive.
Show us the way.
God's law is alive.
Your way is eternal.
God's law is alive.
You law existed before the creation of the universe
God's law is alive.
Your law will be here after the stars burn out.
God's law is alive.
Your way is the only way.
God's law is alive.
Amen.

Outreach/Mission

Jesus said to go into all the world.
We will love like Jesus loved.
Into the big cities and small towns
We will love like Jesus loved.
The farms and mountains
We will love like Jesus loved.
The shelters and homes
We will love like Jesus loved.
Jesus said, "Feed the hungry."
We will love like Jesus loved.
Shelter the homeless
We will love like Jesus loved.
Heal the sick
We will love like Jesus loved.
Visit the imprisoned.
We will love like Jesus loved.
And ask for nothing in return.
We will love like Jesus loved.
Expect nothing in return.
We will love like Jesus loved.
Love without expectation.
We will love like Jesus loved.
Love without strings attached.
We will love like Jesus loved.
It won't be easy.
We will love like Jesus loved.
Some people are hard to love.
We will love like Jesus loved.
It's hard to help those who won't help themselves.
We will love like Jesus loved.
He loved for no other reason than to love.
We will love like Jesus loved.
We will do the same.
We will love like Jesus loved.
Amen.

Patience/Rest

God, we live in a fast world.
We're on your schedule, not ours.
We want what we want when we want it.
We're on your schedule, not ours.
We don't like to wait.
We're on your schedule, not ours.
We are not patient people.
We're on your schedule, not ours.
Too much, too fast, too many.
We're on your schedule, not ours.
Too much to change.
We're on your schedule, not ours.
Too much, too soon.
We're on your schedule, not ours.
Slow us down, God.
We're on your schedule, not ours.
Slow us down, God.
We're on your schedule, not ours.
Fill us with awe and wonder.
We're on your schedule, not ours.
Give us peace.
We're on your schedule, not ours.
The future is out there.
We're on your schedule, not ours.
Let us walk into it as if it were sunshine.
We're on your schedule, not ours.
Not rush into it as if it were a brick wall.
We're on your schedule, not ours.
Our stress cannot add days to our lives.
We're on your schedule, not ours.
Our worry cannot change anything.
We're on your schedule, not ours.
Slow us down, God.
We're on your schedule, not ours.
Slow us down, God.
We're on your schedule, not ours.
We live in a fast world.
We're on your schedule, not ours.
Amen.

Spiritual Gifts

We are like the trees that grow beside the stream. The sunshine and the water feed us and strengthen us.

Fill our hearts with it, God.

Like the fruit on the tree, the fruit of the spirit must grow within us.

Fill our hearts with it, God.

We must give love. Completely. Totally. Without condition.

Fill our hearts with it, God.

We must share the joy that comes from being children of God.

Fill our hearts with it, God.

We must search for peace, in our own minds and in the world.

Fill our hearts with it, God.

We must practice patience. Everything happens in God's time, not ours.

Fill our hearts with it, God.

Kindness and goodness will create a world where no one goes hungry.

Fill our hearts with it, God.

We need to practice faith in order for it to grow.

Fill our hearts with it, God.

Anger can burn down the forest. Gentleness will guide a tree in all seasons.

Fill our hearts with it, God.

With self-control we can make it through any storm.

Fill our hearts with it, God.

This is the fruit of the spirit.

Fill our hearts with it, God.

The time for the harvest has come.

Amen.

Standing Up for What's Right / Temptation

Father, this path has many choices.

There are some places we shouldn't go.

We were hoping it would be easy.

There are some places we shouldn't go.

There should be one path with lots of light.

There are some places we shouldn't go.

We were hoping it would be easy.

There are some places we shouldn't go.

Instead we have lots of opportunities to get lost.

There are some places we shouldn't go.

We see something shiny off to the side.

There are some places we shouldn't go.

We follow the easy trail.

There are some places we shouldn't go.

And before we know it we're stumbling in the dark.

There are some places we shouldn't go.

We've seen the films in school.

There are some places we shouldn't go.

We've seen the commercials.

There are some places we shouldn't go.

We've seen people our age on the news in handcuffs.

There are some places we shouldn't go.

Sooner or later we'll be faced with those choices.

There are some places we shouldn't go.

Why does it look like the bad choice is more fun?

There are some places we shouldn't go.

We will pray to you.

There are some places we shouldn't go.

We will stay on the right path.

There are some places we shouldn't go.

Even though it's really hard sometimes.

There are some places we shouldn't go.

Walk with us.

There are some places we shouldn't go.

Talk with us.

There are some places we shouldn't go.

Because we are aware

There are some places we shouldn't go.

Amen.

Thankfulness /
Understanding /
Inspiration

God, you breathed into the mud and
created man.

Breathe into us, God.

You breathed into Bazalel and gave him
inspiration.

Breathe into us, God.

You chilled the waters and turned them
into ice.

Breathe into us, God.

You turned the seas into dry valleys.

Breathe into us, God.

You created the stars with the wave of
your finger.

Breathe into us, God.

You touched the valley of bones, and the
bones came to life.

Breathe into us, God.

We need life, God.

Breathe into us, God.

This world is suffocating.

Breathe into us, God.

The waters rise up.

Breathe into us, God.

We run so fast we can't even breathe.

Breathe into us, God.

Give us inspiration.

Breathe into us, God.

Give us joy.

Breathe into us, God.

Give us the motivation.

Breathe into us, God.

Give us life.

Breathe into us, God.

Fill us with your holy breath.

Breathe into us, God.

Renew us.

Breathe into us, God.

Renew us.

Breathe into us, God.

Amen.

Private Devotions for Youth Workers

This section is for you! People are *called* into youth ministry because so few sane people would ever *choose* this path. So we heard the call, and here we are. Whether or not your church believes in a "calling," you know God put you where you are. But God didn't say it would be easy. (Why some church folk believe abusing youth workers is a God-given right will remain a mystery until the end of time!)

In the following pages, you will find short devotions written specifically to uplift and guide *you*—especially when you're facing problems, big and small. Each devotion includes Scripture passages. Look them up. Mark them in your Bible. Memorize them if you want.

You'll also find *The Youth Worker's Prayer*. It's written to be repeated the way the Psalms are repeated. Make it part of your daily prayer life. You don't have to memorize it. The more you read it aloud, the more it will feel like your own heart's cry.

The Youth Worker's Prayer

This prayer includes time for you to lift up personal prayers to God.

We encourage you to lift up the names of your students. Say their names out loud. If there's a particular teenager who's in great need, focus your mind on that student's face and his or her problems. Tell God exactly what you want for that teenager. Pray for church members who give you a hard time. Ask God's blessing on them as well. Finally, lift up prayers for you!

I am your servant, God.
Where you want me to go, I will go.
Point the direction. Show me the way.
You called me to work with your young people.
They want to hear your voice, God.
They want to know you.
Help me show them the Creator of the universe.
Send me enthusiasm when I don't feel enthusiastic.
Send me patience when I'm out of it.
Send me large shoulders to lean and cry on.
Send me ears to hear the things that aren't being said.
Send me eyes to see beneath the surface.
Send me words to say when they ask the hard questions.
Give me the ability to laugh at myself.

offer up your students by name
pray for individual students
pray for church members who give you a hard time and don't understand your ministry
pray for your own needs

I am your servant, God.
Where you want me to go, I will go.
Point the direction. Show me the way.
Amen.

"We Gotta Get Outta This Place!"

or, "Gimme One Good Reason Why I Shouldn't Walk Out Right Now!"

Can you relate to this stuff?

Mrs. Fussbudget just stopped by the office to check in with her weekly complaint about what your kids are doing wrong. The music director just scheduled a youth choir practice on the first night of the winter retreat. The treasurer hasn't seen your monthly report. The administrative board wants to look at your goals for the next six years. The senior pastor is worried that you're not spending enough time in your office. A group of parents met last night to compare your performance with the youth pastor you succeeded. An 8th-grade girl talked through your entire Bible study, and your spouse told you as you went out the door, "Don't forget about this weekend!" (And you have no idea what's coming up this weekend, other than you promised a kid you'd go to his school play because he's in the crowd scene.)

What? You can? To all of this stuff??? Then you're definitely a youth worker!

Sometimes it's easy to feel like you do everything in your job except youth ministry. A lot of us become depressed, lost, frustrated, and disconnected.

So what do you do when it all gets to be too much?

Check out these verses

Exodus 20:9-10

Thought: Even if you have to set aside an entire day, do it! Find the time. Take the day off. Unplug the phone. Sit on the couch with your spouse and watch old movies all day. Better yet, get in the car and drive. You don't have to go anyplace special…just go!

Ephesians 5:18

Thought: Is there something you can do to refill the empty glass in your spirit? Is there one song or book or prayer that charges you up? Then save it for times when you're down. Lay it aside. Only bring it out and use it when you need it. Find that special something and make it work for you.

Galatians 6:9

Thought: It's all for God. You're not in this job to please Mrs. Fussbudget or even your senior pastor. You're doing this job to help your teenagers see God in their lives. But don't forget—God is in *your* life, too. It's all going to be okay.

With all your heart, pray this prayer:

Father God, I get so frustrated. Half the time it feels like they don't care, and lately if feels as though I don't, either. Give me compassion, Lord. Give me the patience to deal with the things I need to deal with. Give me the boost so I can keep going. It feels like I'm banging my head against the wall. Give me the strength and wisdom to get over the wall instead of trying to go through it.

I am your servant, Lord. *Amen.*

"Guess What Your Kids Did Now?"
or, "Some people are just never gonna get it. Ever."

You can talk about youth ministry until you're blue in the face. You can write articles for the church newsletter. You can stand on the mountaintops and sing and dance. But some people are just never going to see what you do as "ministry."

To them a game of "Sardines" isn't ministry. And it certainly isn't what they would define as work. (Not work you should get paid for, anyway.) There's a group in your church that believes all children should be "unseen and unheard." Teenagers are just larger children to them. But feel free to parade them out once a year for Youth Sunday and make them available in case the adult Sunday school class needs dishes washed at the pancake breakfast!

"Games? Laughter? At a Bible study? Are you nuts?"

If people don't see what you do as ministry, if they don't recognize the movement of God in your program, they'll criticize you without a second thought.

They have made their tongue as sharp as a serpent's. The poison of vipers is on their lips.— Psalm 140:3

These people don't see the whole story. They don't see you sitting in the crowd at a volleyball game. They don't see you shelling out your own money when kids forgot theirs. They don't see you taking five guys to the burger joint after the Wednesday night Bible study. They don't see that kid reading Scripture around a candle on the winter retreat.

But you do!

What an amazing gift God has given you. What an amazing gift God has given to your students.

God has placed you here for a reason. No, you don't get to know what it is. You just have to trust that there's a reason. Maybe you'll know someday, but for now you just have to go with it. Because your kids give you their trust when they don't trust anyone. They give you their words when they won't talk to anyone.

If you have critics who just don't get what you do, take heart. They'd criticize anyone who'd sit in your office. It's not you. A woman from my old church once told me, "Don't let them get to you. If Jesus himself applied for the job, someone from the church would ask him to get his hair cut before his first day!"

It's not you.

Okay…take a look at Romans 8:17-28.

Thought: Now…you and me and Jesus are there! When you pray today, pray for your critics. Yes, pray for them. Ask God to open their eyes. Ask that they'll see your ministry as ministry. Understand that you probably will never change them. But then again, you aren't here for them anyway, are you?

With all your heart, pray this prayer:

God, why does it seem like so many people are just waiting for me to screw up? Help me keep my tongue in check. I know what I do is ministry. Help me to listen to those who appreciate that fact rather than those who don't. Help me remember that some people have hardened hearts and closed minds. Free them, God. Let them hear the laughter as music, not as noise. Let them see the exuberance of youth as joyful, not as a painful memory. Help me be aware of those around me, God. We are all your children. *Amen.*

"Your Services as Youth Director Are No Longer Required"
or, "Life Begins after You Get Fired"

Remember "The Rock Polisher"? That gizmo from the science section of the toy store? (You know, you put stones in the thing, turn it on for a few days, and out come beautiful polished stones suitable for making jewelry.)

Life is a lot like that.

See, I was fired on a Monday morning. And the funny part? (Well, not ha-ha funny.) While I knew I'd leave that way, it still came as a surprise. I was at an unhealthy church. I was the fifth youth director there in seven years. With more than a decade of youth ministry experience under my belt, I still thought I could turn things around at my new place.

Wrong-o.

I lasted only 17 months. (But hey, that was six months longer than the guy before me!)

I wasn't even fired outright. I was given a "choice." Leave quietly, and they'd give me a check and a reference. Open my mouth, and I get nothing.

I needed the money, so I took the deal.

I lost count of the number of times I asked God, "Why?" during those months. I didn't mind pushing boulders uphill. Sometimes youth ministry is like that. What I minded was all those people on top of the hill pushing those boulders back over me.

Basically it came down to a matter of faith and trust. (And I have to give God credit for knowing more than I did about the plan.)

We don't always get to know what the plan is. We memorize all the cute things to say when it happens to somebody else, but when the "bad stuff" happens to us, we want to fall apart.

The Scriptures are full of people like us. Horrible things happen to them, and later they learn that the "bad stuff" was a refining fire.

We all go through the rock polisher, and it turns us into shiny smooth stones.

- Joseph was beaten by his brothers, tossed into a well, sold, falsely accused of raping his boss's wife, and spent years in prison. From there God placed him in charge of his own empire.
- Daniel was given the choice to pray to the king or pray to God. He prayed to God and was tossed into the lions' den. The lions left him alone.
- Shadrach, Meschach, and Abednego refused to pray to King Nebuchadnezzar's God, and they were tossed into a furnace. The fire didn't burn them.
- Paul was blinded just so he could see the truth. Then he told the truth.
- Jesus...well you know what happened to him.

The fire may burn, but we come out stronger.

Check out these verses

Jeremiah 18:1-6

Numbers 31:23

1 Peter 1:7

Thought: Sometimes we feel like clay pots in the desert. We are cracked and dry. But God is with us. God is there all the time, even if it doesn't feel like it. When we eventually crack and fall apart, God will be there with water. He will reform us. He will let us go through the fire. And we will come out new.

With all your heart, pray this prayer:

Be merciful, God. The fire burns. I am just clay. I will crack and fall apart in your hands. I feel hopeless and hungry. I am frightened of the fire and the water. But you are the potter, and I am the clay. Shape me. Remake me. Mold me in a thousand ways, God. I am your servant. I will be a jar full of glorious treasures. *Amen.*

"They Don't Pay Me Enough for This!"
or, When You Want to Leave

It's one thing to deal with the anger and frustration that comes with the job—but it's quite another thing to sit down and consider whether or not it's time for you to leave.

Sometimes that question will come out of pure frustration. You've tried to implement new programs and new ideas, but you can't get support from the rest of the church. Sometimes it's a matter of growth—you've taken the program as far as you can. Still other times it's another calling—God is ready to move you again.

It will never be an easy decision. Even if you don't get the support you need from your senior pastor or the staff or the church, chances are you've developed some very close relationships with your students.

Those are very hard to leave.

But sometimes you have to.

The question is, "How do you know it's time?"

Ask yourself if you're staying because it's comfortable and safe.

Sometimes we stay where we are because the fear of the unknown is greater than the fear of staying. Anyone who has counseled battered wives will tell you that they continually go back to their abusers because they're afraid to do anything else. It's all they know.

But Peter stood up in the boat. When the rest were hanging on for dear life and throwing up over the side, Peter looked out, saw Jesus, and said, "Lord, if that's really you, invite me out to the water." Jesus said, "Come." And Peter stepped out of the boat.

We all face those moments. Sometimes our churches face storms and other problems. *Do you ever find yourself hanging on for dear life and just hoping to ride out the tempest? Do you feel like you're sailing a storm more often than calm waters?*

If we truly believe God has a purpose for everything, then we must believe God put you into your current situation for a reason. *Do you know what that reason is? Have you come to a sense of completion about certain programs or certain kids?*

Consider this, too.

- The Scriptures are filled with countless references to getting advice from wise counselors. So, what are you waiting for? Talk with your friends in the field. Talk with mentors. Get as much advice and input as you can.

- Make plans in the direction you want to go. If you're in youth ministry now, ask yourself if you want to be in youth ministry 10 years from now. For example, do you want to retire a youth minister? If the answer is "No," then think and pray about where you want to be. Once you start making plans in that direction, God will fill in the blanks. (And check out Proverbs 16:3, 9.)

- If we're working for God, then God has a plan for us. God usually won't close one door without opening another (or at least a window). Look around you. Are there opportunities unfolding?

- Get all the info. You wouldn't fly your students to a far-away missions trip without first making sure they could come back, would you? (Okay, bad example.) In the same way, you wouldn't start building a house without first making sure you can afford to complete it.

- Money is a reality. But just for the sake of argument, take money out of the equation. Check out Ecclesiastes 7:12 and 10:19. Look at all the pros and cons. If money weren't an issue, would you still leave your present position?

- Pray about it. Pray without ceasing. But don't pray for an answer. Pray and tell God, "I am your servant!" God will hear you. God will place you where you should go. (Check out James 1:5.)

- It's right to put your problem in Jesus' hands—only remember that God gave you two hands as well! If you want a new position, it's probably not going to come looking for you. So get crackin' and update your resume. Make phone calls. If God wants you in a new place, he'll put you in a new place. Open yourself up to the possibilities, and God will be there.

"Should I stay or should I go?" It's one of the most important decisions of your life. Give it that kind of importance when you consider the answer.

With all your heart, pray this prayer:

God, I am your servant. Sometimes I think I'm going crazy. I love these kids so much, and yet I don't know if I can stay here anymore. Show me the way, God. Hold my hand as I walk this path. Let me know that I'm not alone. Let me be certain in my decision. Let my choice glorify your name. *Amen.*

"I'm Sick and Tired of This Job!"
or, When It's Your Turn to Complain

Do you remember *Monty Python?* That great, old British show with the lunatic comedians? One of their classic sketches is called "The Argument Clinic." In it, a customer pays to have an argument. When the argument doesn't go well, the customer storms down the hall and finds the door marked "Complaints." The customer bursts in and yells, "I want to complain!"

The man behind the desk replies, "You want to complain? Look at these shoes. I've only had them a week and the heels are worn right through. Oh, my back hurts! It's not a very fine day. I'm sick and tired of this office." And on and on.

Sound familiar? We may very well have reason to complain. Ours isn't the most glamorous job, is it? We have wondrous ideas for programs and retreats and youth talks, and then we get shot down. We find out the day before the Couples Pancake Breakfast that the students were "volunteered" to wash the dishes. The church van can't travel more than 100 miles without breaking down, but instead of getting it fixed, the board's decision is, "Just do more local events." No one seems to care!

You can list your complaints. So can I. And if we put your list together with my list and the lists of everyone else who's reading these words, we'd have a list that would stretch to the moon and back again.

Do you know what we would have then?

A lot of paper (but I digress).

It seems most of us go about complaining in one of two ways:

1. Loudly and constantly.

2. Quietly and kindly.

Usually neither method will get you what you're truly after. Oh sure, the squeaky wheel often gets the grease, but when it keeps squeaking, eventually it gets replaced. And seldom will it be the only one replaced. The mechanic will replace other parts while on the job.

Other people will sit and say nothing—or say something to the wrong somebody. If the restaurant put mustard on your burger when you asked them to hold it, do you send it back or quietly scrape it off with your knife and eat the burger anyway?

There's nothing wrong with asking to get what you pay for. If the service isn't what it should be, offer that info to the server or the manager.

But when we begin finding fault with everything, that's when things really start to fall apart.

Think about what happens when you complain. Like the *Monty Python* sketch, usually others respond with complaints of their own. It spreads like the flu. And soon everyone around you has caught it, and nothing is getting done.

Two Magic Words

The two most potent magic words are **not** *abra* and *cadabra*. (They're not even *ala* and *kazamm*.) They are *therefore* and *however*.

Why?

Well, if you catch yourself complaining or if your meeting begins sliding into a complaint session, invoke these two words by saying, "Okay. From now on, no one is allowed to offer a complaint of any kind unless you're willing to add the words *however* or *therefore*, and then keep talking."

In other words: "We can't get any funds for new athletic equipment, *however*…"

"The kids are getting tired of pizza every Sunday night, *therefore*…"

You'll be amazed at how quickly the complaints can become constructive—or at least taper off.

So, in your own ministry, don't offer complaints unless you can offer methods of improving the situations.

In Psalm 142:2, David says he "lays his complaints before the Lord before I tell him my trouble." What's the difference between complaining and being a complainer? David seems to get it all out of his system and then asks God for help in specific situations.

Usually the complaint is very general: "We can never do what we want!"

More specifically it may be, "Mrs. Fussbudget doesn't like us to use the kitchen on Sundays."

God wants his children to be happy. He gives us amazing gifts. Yet when we see the ocean, we tend to focus on the seaweed. When we see the beautiful autumn leaves, we see the mess they make.

Focus on what's good. If your youth room is too small, thank God for you have one. If your books and curriculum are dated, thank God for your ability to be creative.

Paul says we, as the teachers of God's kingdom, are to do all things without complaining (Philippians 2:14-16). Because we are, in fact, examples to the world. We should be like shining stars in the universe. We know we are role models for our teens. Maybe if we find less to complain about, they our students will, too.

With all your heart, pray this prayer:

God, maybe it's time I stop trying to put everything into your hands and use the two that you gave me. I thank you for all the blessings you've added to my life. Forgive me for complaining about the things I don't have. Help me focus my heart on what is good about my life and my ministry. I know all things come from you. You will take what's good and what's bad and make them work together. Thank you, God. *Amen.*

"You Say 'Tomato,' I Say 'The Glass Is Half Empty'"
or, "Everybody Has an Opinion"

If you've been in youth ministry more than a year, you already know the one question you should never ask: "What do you want on your pizza?"

Nothing will kick off an argument quicker. The meat eaters and the vegetarians will square off immediately. Then you have the "just cheese" crowd. And then there's always the one kid who likes pineapple.

It's amazing how we let differing opinions rattle us. Churches have split over whether or not to use *debts* or *trespasses* in the Lord's Prayer. Churches have divided over contemporary versus traditional worship—until we get to the point where we have two churches sharing the same building. Arguing is one thing, but when we argue in church, we tend to dig our heels in and act as if God's on our side.

Many hold fast to their beliefs because of history. If our students have washed the dishes for the pancake breakfast for the last 10 years, then "that is the way God wants it!" (Incidentally, two years makes a tradition…three years makes a rut. If you have a wildly successful fundraiser or program, don't run it more than two years in a row, or you'll be doing it until you retire.)

Winning the argument versus find the solution

We want to win. Sometimes at the expense of a solution, we want to win that argument. Spouses nag each other until one concedes. Parents harp on their children until they clean their rooms. These are not solutions. These are imposing one set of opinions over others by unfair means. If you're in a disagreement with others, it's okay to stick to your guns if they're obviously just trying to get their way instead of working out a reasonable solution. By the same token, however, don't push yourself on others that way. They're children of God, too.

They Are?

People who don't agree with us are not our enemies. It's easy for youth workers to make enemies. Teenagers are messy, nosy, they slouch, they use "that word." But those who line up outside your pastor's office to complain about you are, believe it or not, God's special children.

Treat them as such. Encourage your teens to speak to their biggest detractors as if they are God's chosen. You may not get the same treatment in return, but don't let that stop you. God is in charge, not you.

"Waiter, There's a Camel In My Soup!"

You blind guides! You strain out a gnat but swallow a camel. —Matthew 23:24

I love this verse. It's one of those unforgettable passages where Jesus finally had enough and let the Pharisees have it.

We take so much time fussing about little details that we miss the big picture. We argue to the death about the color of the new carpet in the sanctuary. We sit as far away as possible from a person we're arguing with. We spend hours, days, and weeks building up our position—and then we miss the visitor who just came and went from our service without so much as a "welcome." (And why would that visitor want to stay, anyway?)

Tomato, tom*ato*…it's still God's salad.

Check out Romans 14:5-6.

Thought: Paul says that we all believe differently. Right down to the very nature of God, we will disagree on things. What's important is that we do everything *for* God. You may believe a certain way, but make sure you're believing that way for God's sake, not yours—and not for the people in line outside the pastor's office.

With all your heart, pray this prayer:

Creator, give me ears to hear those who don't agree with me. Remind me in a very clear way that we're all in this together. Wrestling with someone in a lifeboat will only drown us all. Let me see all sides, all the angles, and all the solutions. Help me find the solution you want and not make others angry, pushing for my own way. Help me find the solution and not roll over and give in because my meeting runs late or I just get tired. *Amen.*

"Is Pizza, Soda Pop, and Chips Really the Breakfast of Champions?"

or, "When You Think You're Getting Too Old for This"

It hit me several years ago. I took a group of students to an amusement park where I used to go as a teenager. When I was 15, I could run that park from one end to the other. Now I was the one who stood there with the chaperones, studying the park map, and figuring we should see the Mega Movie in the afternoon when it got hot. I was the one looking at my watch and saying, "Gee, only six more hours 'til we go home."

The glory of young men is in their strength. The honor of old men is in their gray hair.—Proverbs 20:29

So what if you used to play volleyball or shoot baskets and now you just blow the whistle? You aren't too old for this! If God called you to youth ministry, don't you think your getting older is part of the plan? Eventually you have to move from being a player to being a coach.

There are many roles in youth ministry. *Older* does not necessarily mean *mature*. By the time you've passed a decade in youth ministry, you know all the good lines. You can come up with those weird ideas. You can spot a prank coming a mile away. There are advantages to the gray hair. You have a tremendous amount of experience. You can offer advice on just about any subject.

Youth Specialties has several conventions each year. One of the opening games is to find out who's been in youth ministry the longest. Five thousand people all stand up. The leader onstage begins calling out numbers: 2, 4, 6…and when he reaches the number of years you've been in youth ministry, you're asked to sit down. One year, it came down to a smiling, gray-haired woman standing in the back of the room. She said she'd been in youth ministry for 47 years! As a volunteer, no less!

If you feel God is calling you elsewhere, then by all means, follow that call. But never let "I'm too old for this" be a deciding factor.

Solomon said, "That which has been is that which will be, and that which has been done is that which will be done. So, there is nothing new under the sun." The beauty of this calling is that we're constantly bombarded by what's new. Teenagers will always be showing you what's new in music, clothing, technology, and faith.

My students constantly surprise me. Just when I think it's all the same, they come up with something that just blows me out of the water.

When we start out, we all want to be Luke Skywalker. We want to fight the Dark Side and swing across the pit. Then eventually we become Obi Won. We are the teachers. We are the sages. We are the wise and knowledgeable.

And someday…Yoda!

With all your heart, pray this prayer

God, it hurts to play volleyball. Pizza gives me indigestion. And sleeping on the floor gives me a backache. So thank you for coffee. Thank you for antacid tablets. Most of all, thank you for the wonderful laughter and energy of teenagers who keep me from becoming old. Let me feel their energy. Let me learn from them. Keep me smart enough to keep up with what's going on in their lives. Give me the answer when they ask me the hard questions. Sustain me on this path, God. Send your son to encourage me so that I may encourage others. *Amen.*

Communion/Worship Service for Eucharist CD

This service follows the *Eucharist* CD exactly. It calls for both spontaneous dancing and silence. It requires a great deal of preparation, but the end result is well worth it!

Supplies

Boom box, *Eucharist* CD, handouts with lyrics to track 4, "Holy Holy Holy" and track 7, "I Believe," poster board/butcher paper printed with lyrics of the second and third stanzas of track 2, "Hush," paper lunch bags, pens, pencils, blank paper, large sheet of butcher paper, finger paint (various colors), drop cloth, paint brushes, wet wipes, candles, communion elements, straps of soft leather to make bracelets

Preparation

1. Hold the first track, "House of the Lord," outside of the worship area if possible. The worship area should be should be dark, illuminated only by candles. (You can bring the lights up slightly during times when students need to read the lyrics to the hymns. The candles should be burning when the students enter during "Hush.")

2. Place the poster board with the lyrics to "Hush" on the door of the worship area.

3. Hang a large sheet of butcher paper inside the worship area. You'll need at least two adult volunteers in this area to prevent messes. Place the drop cloth on the floor beneath the butcher paper. Put the finger paint in small bowls. The adult volunteers will paint your students' palms and fingers. After your students have printed an "angel" on the paper, a second adult will hand them wet wipes for quick clean up.

4. Copy the instructions for "Confession and Gifts" found on page 124. Attach one sheet to each lunch bag. Be ready to hand these out to students, along with pens or pencils, during track 5, "Kyrie."

5. Have the communion elements ready, but do not prepare them for the service until track 8, "Pray."

6. The soft leather straps are necessary to make "bindings" (bracelets). Do not make these ahead of time. It's much more dramatic and moving if you create them on the spot. Because of time constraints, you may need several adult volunteers creating these at the same time. Don't make them too long. Cut off any excess length, too, as some teens like to wear the bracelets for a long time.

The Worship Service

Before the service gather your group together and say something like, "Much of this service is done in silence. A variety of activities will take place during the service, and there will not be time for instructions. You have to pay close attention so you know what's going on."

Explain also that they'll be receiving communion at their seats or by coming forward. Do communion in a different way than they're used to. Try using real unleavened bread. If you have a larger group, you may need several communion stations.

Begin worship

Leader: God calls us all to let go of the chains and restrictions we place on ourselves. David danced without embarrassment before God. He didn't care what people thought because his dance was for the Lord. We will begin this service with dancing. You can move any way you'd like, but don't focus on what others are doing. Focus on God. Focus on worshiping him with your whole body.

Play track 1, "House of the Lord"

When the song ends, gather your group in front of the door to the worship area. (By this time, the worship area is dark and illuminated by candles. This is a nice "calming" effect when the doors open.) Pass out the bulletins they'll be using later.

Play track 2, "Hush"

Have the kids read along with the printed lyrics. When the CD says "fling open the doors"…do that! And let your group enter the worship area and be seated.

Before you play track 3, "Angel," wait for silence. Demonstrate (in silence) the next part of the service. Have the worship leader walk to the "paint" station and place his/her hands together by meeting the thumbs.

Have the adult volunteer paint the worship leader's hands. The worship leader will "make an angel" on the butcher paper. (Be sure your kids see the leader wash his/her hands with the wet wipe and place it in the trash!)

Play track 3, "Angel"

While "Angel" is playing, motion for your students to stand and then lead them in a line to the paint station. (You may need to play track 3 several times depending on the size of your group. You also may want to hang the "angel" banner in your youth room after the service.)

Play track 4, "Holy Holy Holy"

Have the group use their bulletins so they can sing along. After the hymn, pass out the paper lunch bags (with the instruction sheets attached to each one) and pencils (silently).

Play tracks 5 and 6, "Kyrie" and "Gloria"

This portion of the service includes a confession. Assure your students that their words will be private by personally removing the bags from the altar after the service and either burning them or throwing them away discreetly.

When your students return to their seats, move to the next phase of the service.

Play track 7, "I Believe"

Have your students sing along using the lyrics printed on the bulletin.

Preparing the Eucharist

Play track 8, "Pray," and prepare the worship table in silence.

Play track 9, "Eucharistic Prayer," and have your students receive communion.

You may or may not be able to match your actions to the disc depending on the size of your group.

Allow the CD to continue into track 10, "I Will Receive You Now."

Closing

Play track 11, "Breastplate"

As the song plays, lead the group forward in single-file line (like you did with track 3, "Angel"). Have adult volunteers tie leather bracelets around the students' wrists. Don't tie the bracelets so tightly that your students lose circulation! A simple knot will hold the strap in place. A pair of scissors will take off the excess.

Closing Prayer

Leader: God, today we bind ourselves to you. We are your children. You forgive us all the things we have done and things that we have left undone. You have given us gifts beyond our comprehension. You have shown us the way to you through your son, Jesus Christ. Go with us now. Be a light on our path. Walk beside us. Hold our hands. Let us feel your presence as we go from this place and into the world you have created for us. *Amen.*

Instructions for "Confession and Gifts"
(track 5, "Kyrie")

A Time for Confession and Thanks

Take the blank sheet of paper, and on one side quickly write down all the things you want God to forgive you for. It could be harsh words you exchanged with your parents. It could be something you said or did to a friend at school. No one will see this except you and God. Take about 60 seconds to do this now.

On the opposite side of the paper, write down all the things you're good at—art, sports, listening to music, math, skateboarding…anything you want to note. It doesn't matter how trivial you think these things are; they're all gifts from God. Take about 60 seconds to do this now.

Place the sheet in the paper bag and fold the top down. Don't put your name on the bag—your leader will discard or destroy all the bags after the service.

Say a prayer asking God's forgiveness for the things you want forgiveness for, and also say a prayer thanking God for all the gifts he's given you.

When you're done, carry the bag forward and place it on the altar.

Lyrics and Notes for Eucharist CD

1. House of the Lord

2. Hush

Welcome to our worship we're
celebrating the Eucharist
God the creator is a gracious, abundant
and generous host
You are invited to be guests at his table

Grace and peace to you from him
Who was and is and is to come
And from the seven spirits before his
throne
And from Jesus Christ who is the faithful
witness
The firstborn from the dead
And the ruler of the kings of the earth

Eternal God
Fling open the doors of our hearts
To the weather of your Spirit
Lead us out beneath the dancing sky and
wind
Across the stumbling ground of our
reality
To where the sound of worship never
ceases
And the view stretches further than the
human eye can see
Through Christ the faithful witness
Amen

Relax
God is here

3. Angel

Seven golden lamps are shining ANGEL
Where the Son of Man goes walking
ANGEL
Calling out for us to hear him ANGEL
Calling out to seven churches ANGEL

Sing praise to Christ our God (4X)

Eyes that burn like fire flying ANGEL
Words that sound like rushing rivers
ANGEL
In his hands are seven bright stars
ANGEL
In his face the sun is shining ANGEL

I am Alpha and Omega ANGEL
I was crucified and broken ANGEL

Now I am alive forever ANGEL
Death can never stop my living ANGEL

Do you understand the mystery ANGEL
What is now and what will happen
ANGEL
Seven stars are seven angels ANGEL
Seven lamps are seven churches ANGEL

4. Holy holy holy

Holy holy holy Lord God Almighty
Early in the morning our song shall rise
to thee
Holy holy holy Merciful and mighty
God in three persons blessed Trinity

Holy holy holy all the saints adore thee
Casting down their golden crowns
around the glassy sea
Cherubim and seraphim falling down
before thee
Who was and is and evermore shall be

Holy holy holy through the darkness
hide thee
Though the sinful human eye thy glory
may not see
Only thou art holy there is none beside
thee
Perfect in power in love and purity

Holy holy holy Lord God Almighty
All thy works shall praise thy name in
earth and sky and sea
Holy holy holy merciful and mighty
God in three persons blessed Trinity

5. Kyrie

Kyrie eleison
Christe eleison
Lord have mercy
Christ have mercy

Holy God accept our confession
You asked for all of our being
Our thoughts and actions, our creativity
and expression
What do we give you?
We think back two millennia to when
the Christ child was born
What would we give the baby?
What does the baby ask of us?
What gifts did the baby receive?

Gold – a gift for a king
A metal so precious that we have died
and killed for it
We treat your creation like it wasn't our
home
We've robbed the earth of its riches
And left its wounds open to infection
Forgive us for not unwrapping your gift
to us in the right spirit
Forgive us for not giving you the best of
us
What's the point of offering you the
religious bits
If the rest is kept closely guarded?

Kyrie elesion
Christe elesion
Lord have mercy
Christ have mercy

Frankincense – a gift for God
The fragrance of worship, God's eau de
cologne
Worship giving God the honour that is
due to him
We saw your creation as a dirty thing
That we had to manufacture souls for
heaven
Forgive our efforts to worship you
Only when it is convenient to do so
And with people that we choose making
outcasts of our brothers and sisters
Forgive us when our actions make our
Words of worship meaningless

Kyrie elesion
Christe elesion
Lord have mercy
Christ have mercy

Myrrh – a gift for a mortal
The smell of a cover up to hide death
and decay
But nothing is hidden from you
Forgive us for denying the reality of pain
suffering and struggle
Do we get angry and shout at God?
Or do we bury our pain?
Forgive us for not giving our pain and
suffering to you
And for not interceding for others

Kyrie elesion
Christe elesion
Lord have mercy
Christ have mercy
You ask for all that we are

What do we give?
May we take seriously the meaning of
Your birth and your cross
Amen

6. Gloria

Glory to God in the highest
God's peace on the earth
Lord God Heavenly King
Almighty God and Father
We worship you we give you thanks
We praise you for your glory

Lord Jesus Christ only Son of God
Lord God lamb of God
You take away the sin of the world
Have mercy on us all
You sit at God's right hand on high
Receive our prayer today

For you alone are the holy one
You are the only Lord
You alone are God most high
You are Jesus Christ
You are with the Holy Spirit
In the Father's glory

Glory to God Alleluia
Amen Alleluia

7. I believe

I believe in God the Father Almighty
I believe that he made the earth and
heavens
I believe in Jesus born of a woman
I believe that he is the Son of God

I believe
I believe I believe I believe I believe I
believe
I believe I believe I believe I believe I
believe

I believe in Jesus teacher and healer
I believe that his life was poor and
simple
I believe he died betrayed and rejected
I believe that he fought the power of evil

I believe the holy life-giving Spirit
Is a gift of the Son and Father to us
I believe the three are one and united
I believe in his healing and forgiveness
I believe that Jesus died and was buried
I believe that he rose to life again

I believe that he was taken to heaven
I believe that he reigns at God's right
hand

I believe that he will come back in glory
I believe that he will judge the dead and
living
I believe the resurrection of body
I believe in the life that's everlasting

8. Pray

Let us pray
Lord in your mercy hear our prayer

9. Eucharistic Prayer

The Lord is here
His Spirit is with us
Lift up your hearts

We lift them to God
Let us give thanks to the Lord our God
It is right to give him thanks and praise

O Lord our God sustainer of the universe
At your command all things came to be
The vast expanse of interstellar space
Galaxies suns the planets in their
courses
And this fragile earth our island home
By your will they were created and have
their being

Redeemer God word become flesh
We remember you in bread and wine
Your body your blood
Broken so we with all creation may be
made perfect
Through your sacrifice death is nulled
Through your resurrection we have a
future
Thank you

Therefore with angels and animals
Microbes and mountains
And all that lives for you
We proclaim how wonderful you are
We pour out our thanks to you
In song that never sleeps

Holy holy holy Lord
God of power and might
Heaven and earth are full of your glory
Hosanna in the highest

And now we ask that by the power of

your Holy Spirit
This bread and wine may be to us
Christ's body and his blood
Who on the night that he was handed
over
To suffering and death
Took bread thanked you and broke it
He gave it to his friends saying
"Eat this it is my body given for you do
this in memory of me"
Later after supper he took the cup
Thanked you and gave it to them saying
"Drink this all of you this is my blood of
the new covenant
Which is shed for you and for many for
the forgiveness of sins
Do this whenever you drink it in
memory of me"

Christ has died
Christ is risen
Christ will come again

In this place where heaven and earth
meet
Under the rainbow of God's promise
In this sharing of bread and wine
Future hope becomes reality now

So bring your scorched earth
Bring your harvest
Bring your open sky
Bring your restless guilty waters
Bring your swift unbending road
Bring your urgent inner city
To the table where your host says
"I make all things new"

Lamb of God you take away the sin of
the world
Have mercy on us

10. I will receive you now

Come and be here
Steal past my fears
O wounded healer
O humble leader
Show me your hands
Show me your side
O holy victim
O crucified

I will receive you now
I will receive your love
I will believe in you
I will go on with you

Speak to my heart
Bring me your peace
O broken Saviour
O gentle fighter

Breathe on my face
The breath of life
O my Christ let me
Share in your life

Bring to my lips no
Your blood and boc
O bread of heaven
O hope of glory
Send me in love
Into the world
O faithful teacher
Wisdom of God

11. Breastplat

All saving God
Thank you for feed
and blood
Of your son Jesus
Whose death and
Purchased the futu
We who have taste
Kingdom
Offer ourselves as
In the power of yo
And as lovers and
you have made
Until you come
Amen, come Lord J

I bind unto myself
The strong name of the trinity
By invocation of the same
The three in one and one in three

I bind unto myself today
The great love of the living word
The wisdom of my God to teach
His hand to guide his shield to ward

I bind unto myself today
The virtues of the starlit heaven
The glorious sun's life giving ray
The fruits of earth so freely given

I bind unto myself today
The power of God to hold and lead
His eye to watch his might to stay
His ear to hearken to my need

I bind unto myself today
The way of Christ in the life and death
The call of God to jubilee
In broken chains and cancelled debt

Go in peace

, Third
ice

ve Collins

Baker and

r (1783-

3-76)

Birch, and

ly Thornton
Music)

trick

(lyrics reprinted by permission)